101
Ways to
CAPTIVATE
a
Business
Audience

101
Ways to
CAPTIVATE
a
Business
Audience

SUE GAULKE

amacom
American Management Association
New York • Atlanta • Boston • Chicago • Kansas City • San Francisco • Washington, D.C.
Brussels • Mexico City • Tokyo • Toronto

This book is available at a special
discount when ordered in bulk quantities.
For information, contact Special Sales Department,
AMACOM, a division of American Management Association,
1601 Broadway, New York, NY 10019

This publication is designed to provide accurate and authoritative
information in regard to the subject matter covered. It is sold with the
understanding that the publisher is not engaged in rendering legal,
accounting, or other professional service. If legal advice or other expert
assistance is required, the services of a competent professional person
should be sought.

Library of Congress Cataloging-in-Publication Data

Gaulke, Sue.
        101 ways to captivate a business audience / Sue Gaulke.
            p.   cm.
        Includes index.
        ISBN 0-8144-7920-0
        1. Business communication.   2. Business presentations.   3. Public
speaking.   I. Title.
        HF5718.G38   1996
        658.4'5—dc20   96-32669
                                                                               CIP

Printing number

10   9   8   7   6   5   4   3   2

Dedicated

to **Scott,** my number 1 fan
to **Lindsey,** who keeps me thinking
to **Lauren,** who keeps me laughing

Contents

List of the 101 Ways   ix

Preface   xiii

Acknowledgments   xv

Part One   Steak   **1**

1 Your Audience Speaks   3
2 Connect With Your Audience   13
3 Steak: Organization Made Easy   24

Part Two   Sizzle   **39**

4 Add Sizzle Every Six Minutes   41

Part Three   Style   **51**

5 Control Nervousness: The *Star Wars* Theory   53
6 Style: Becoming a "10"   62
7 Master the Magic in Your Voice   74
8 Create Exciting Visual Aids   85
9 Bulletproof Your Presentation   99
10 Stupid Meetings? Try Some Steak, Sizzle, and Style   110
11 This Stuff Really Works   123

Conclusion   127

**Part Four   Standing Ovation: Quick Tips and
            Resources**   **129**

Camp Chat: Answers to the Most Frequently Asked
             Questions   131

Quick Tips   142

Recommended Resources   149

Index   151

List of the 101 Ways

1. Listen to Your Audience   5
2. Captivate With *Steak, Sizzle,* and *Style*   6
3. Work Harder on Your *Sizzle* and *Style*   7
4. Avoid the Ten Terrible Turn-offs   7
5. Be Creative With Both Technical and Nontechnical
   Audiences   9
6. Audiences Want Steak: Know Your Stuff   10
7. Audiences Want Sizzle: Be Interesting   10
8. Audiences Want Style: Be Enthusiastic   11
9. Know Your Audience   14
10. Find An Informant   14
11. Step Into Their Shoes   15
12. Get in Synch With Your Audience   17
13. Become an Insider   18
14. Activate Their "On" Buttons   18
15. Enhance Your Charisma Factor   19
16. Develop Your OOMPH   20
17. Reach Into Their Souls   21
18. Tame the Troublemakers   22
19. Think Like a Kid: Jump-Start Your Presentation   25
20. Spin an Idea Web   25
21. Plan for Steak and Sizzle   27
22. Create a Clear Focus   29
23. Select Three to Five Main Points (the Body)   30
24. Jazz Up the Main Points   31
25. GRABM With a Great Introduction   32
26. Make Your Summary Memorable   33
27. Check the Sizzle Supply   34

28. Storyboard Your Ideas   34
29. Scoop and Deliver: Keep Your Notes Simple   35
30. Anchor Your Message   36
31. Plan for Persuasion   37
32. Use Stories and Examples   42
33. Quote an Interesting or Unusual Authority   43
34. Show-and-Tell (Demonstrate a Product or Idea)   44
35. Find Common Ground With Your Audience   44
36. Dazzle Them With Props   46
37. Use Strategic Name Dropping   46
38. Self-Disclose (the Whoops Factor)   47
39. Showcase Your Hobby   48
40. Activate Your Audience: Involve Them   49
41. Make Them Laugh   50
42. Never Say "Nervous"   54
43. Think Positive Thoughts   54
44. Behave Like a Duck   55
45. Soothe Your Symptoms   56
46. Relax   57
47. Prepare! Prepare! Prepare!   57
48. Focus on the Audience—Not on Yourself   58
49. Don't Panic   59
50. Eat Like an Athlete   60
51. Exercise   60
52. Remember That *You* Are Number 1 With the
    Audience   62
53. Look Like a "10"—for Men   63
54. Look Like a "10"—for Women   65
55. Communicate Eyeball to Eyeball   67
56. Take Up Space   68
57. Don't Get Stuck   69
58. Avoid Fiddling, Fidgeting, and Flagrant Fouls   70
59. Show Your Glow (Smile!)   71
60. Stretch Your Style   72
61. Evaluate Your Style   73
62. Breathe Low and Slow   75
63. Check the Speed Limit   76
64. Trash Your Vocal Garbage   77
65. Pitch It Low and Wide   78

66. Gauge Your Gusto 79
67. Pause to Punctuate a Point 80
68. Speak From Your Heart 81
69. Change the Beat 82
70. Develop Your Vocal Uniqueness 83
71. Take Good Care of Your Voice 84
72. Create Simple Visuals 86
73. Avoid the Tiny-Cluttered-Numbers Syndrome 86
74. Keep Your Visuals Visible 87
75. Add Spontaneous Flair With Flip Charts 88
76. Supercharge Your Overhead Transparencies 90
77. Control Your Overhead Show 91
78. Electrify Your Presentation: Videos, Slides,
    Computer-Generated Shows 92
79. Reinforce Details With Handy Handouts 95
80. Test! Test! And Test Again! 96
81. Glow, Even When the Lights Go Out 97
82. Check the Pulse 100
83. Pinpoint the Problem 101
84. Recover: Take a Break 102
85. Recover: End Early 103
86. "Up" Your Energy Level 104
87. Get Up and Boogie 105
88. Lose the Notes 106
89. Step Out of the Spotlight: Involve the Group 107
90. Change Pace: Do Something Different 107
91. Pack Some Ideas Into Your Hip Pocket 108
92. Say No to Meetings 111
93. Meeting Steak: Cut the Fat 112
94. Keep It Quick and Snappy: Twenty-Five Steps to a
    Fifty-Nine-Minute Meeting 112
95. Keep on Track With the Fifty-Nine-Minute
    Meeting Guide 114
96. Gather Your Guts: Evaluate Your Meeting 114
97. Have Fun! Add Meeting Sizzle 116
98. Assign a Cast of Characters 117
99. Become a Fantastic Facilitator 118
100. Waltz Through Sticky Situations 119
101. Rate Your Meeting Style 121

Preface

The following is a *true* story. It was a crummy Thursday morning in the spring of 1986. I was driving home from an early morning business meeting in Portland, Oregon. It was a typical spring day in Oregon—lots of rain, with an occasional sun break. I was feeling just as crummy as the weather. How was a trainer stuck in a tiny corner of the United States ever going to make it "big time"? After about eight miles of feeling sorry for myself, a rainbow appeared. Holy cow! In fact, I was at the end of the rainbow. The rainbow was right over my car, and a piece of the rainbow was outside the passenger window. If someone had been sitting in the passenger's seat, he or she could have stuck an arm out of the window and touched the rainbow. I couldn't help but think, "Yes! The pot of gold must be coming!" For the next few minutes I felt as though I were in a fantasy land. The rainbow continued to hover around my car. I knew that something special was going to happen that day.

And it did. Fifty miles later, as I turned off at my exit, the gold started to shine. It was on the north side of the road—an old hotel, so classy and majestic that I imagined people coming from all over the world to train with me there. I would become so famous that people would be willing to fly to this tiny corner of the United States. That evening I read an article about a trainer in the South who was training businesspeople in presentation skills. That was exactly what I wanted to do! I already had a similar program that I presented once each year to our regional phone company. That was my favorite workshop. Why not expand it and market it nationwide to the top corporations in the country? Gold! I found it!

I called it the Speakers Training Camp, and for the last ten years I have presented it worldwide to companies large and small. I still offer one session here in the Northwest each year, but I have extended my workshop sites all around the country. I call it a camp because it's fun, it's practical, and, just as at a sports camp, the more "at bats" you have, the better you become. For years, my clients have been begging me to put the ideas taught in the camp into a book. You are about to read the results of those labors. If you are interested in finding out about the Speakers Training Camp, feel free to write to me c/o the publisher, AMACOM, 1601 Broadway, New York, NY 10019-7606.

This book is designed to help you become an extraordinary presenter—in the top 5 percent. I want to teach you the skills that will help you to become your own best coach for long-term improvement, and to have fun giving presentations.

I wanted to bring you the best information possible, so I decided to ask audiences some questions about what they like and don't like about presenters. Their responses formed the basis of this book. Now you'll know, from the people who really count: your audience—the people signing the contracts, buying the products, and closing the deals. What they say is very clear. Boring speakers don't go to heaven: they don't win applause, make the sales, or win the contracts.

I hope you enjoy the book. I hope you take some risks and try some new ideas. I found the pot of gold, but it's more fun to spread it around to people like you!

Sue Gaulke

Acknowledgments

Thanks and appreciation to Davinne McKeown-Ellis, Ann Matejko, Dan Poynter, Dianna Booher, Micki Chapman, my agent Jeff Herman, and Mary Glenn of AMACOM.

Thanks to my golf buddies at Hood River Golf and Country Club and Indian Creek Golf for keeping me in the right frame of mind.

Special appreciation to the following reviewers and contributors:

Kenneth Forrester, computer trainer and software developer, Tony's Pizza, Salina, Kansas

Bill O'Hearn, founder of the Alpha Institute for Human Possibilities, speaker, and author, Wilsonville, Oregon

Jan Graham, corporate training coordinator for First Commercial Corporation, Little Rock, Arkansas

Steve Hewitt, past director of continuing legal education, Oregon State Bar, Lake Oswego, Oregon

Michael Smith, director of training, Boat/U.S., Alexandria, Virginia

Jean Watson, training consultant and president of Watson & Associates, Tyler, Texas

Betty Osborne, communications administrator, Sprint/United Telephone of the Northwest, Hood River, Oregon

Mary Donnelly, training and development specialist, Country Companies, Bloomington, Illinois

Buddy Howell, training supervisor, Department of Health & Welfare, State of Idaho, Caldwell, Idaho

Barbara Ryan Church, Ed.D., former television news anchorwoman who is currently an organizational psychologist for the U.S. government, Glynco, Georgia

John Dailey, writer, editor, training consultant, and speaker; president of Human Potential Unlimited, Inc., McLean, Virginia

Part One
Steak

Chapter 1
Your Audience Speaks

I always sit in the quick-exit seats, the ones right by the door. When I attend a presentation, I want the option of escaping the clutches of a boring speaker who's wasting my time. I'm amazed at the number of people who will politely sit in their seats, trapped by a speaker from hell. Their minds scream, "Shut up!" while their bodies fidget in disgust.

Early in my career as a presentation skills coach, I was asked to provide some one-day programs for the Oregon State Bar Continuing Legal Education speakers. These were lawyers who were presenting programs to their peers. To research the task, and to find out all about these programs, I attended one of the organization's standard training sessions. Approximately 350 attorneys were seated behind rows of tables at the Hilton Hotel in downtown Portland, Oregon. You couldn't see many faces, because most of the attendees were reading their morning newspapers. The news must have been really captivating that day, because when the speaker started to talk, most of the newspapers remained in their upright positions. Wait a minute; something's out of place here, I thought. The speaker has begun, and most of the audience is ignoring him. And if that's not enough, the speaker is ignoring their apparent total lack of interest.

My mission for this organization, and for the remainder of my professional life, became quite clear. I would train presenters to be so outstanding that in a setting like this, those newspapers would come crashing down. My job would be to help speakers captivate the audience and hold their attention right up to the closing line.

Defining a Strategy

I had a lot of questions. By what magic can people hold an audience spellbound? I was interested in the best. What's different about the top 5 percent? What presentation pitfalls must be avoided? How could I find the answers and then teach the required skills to my clients? I distilled my curiosity into three questions, given in Figure 1-1, which I posed to over 1,000 businesspeople throughout the United States. In this chapter, you will learn the secrets of spectacular speakers—from the audience's viewpoint. Their simplicity might surprise you!

The audiences represented a wide variety of occupations, including certified public accountant, engineer, company vice president, sales director, hairdresser, pilot, dentist, programmer,

Figure 1-1. Audience survey questionnaire.

Spectacular Speaker Survey

1. Who is the most memorable speaker you have ever heard? (speaker, presenter, trainer, any type of speaker)

   _____

2. What is it about this person that makes him or her so outstanding? (try to list three qualities)

   _____

   _____

   _____

3. What is the worst thing a speaker can do to turn you off, bug you, even make you grind your teeth in agony?

   _____

technical writer, financial analyst, pharmacist, secretary, and health care technician.

I administered the questionnaire at the beginning of the session, before the audience had a chance to be influenced by my training. I elaborated on the first question, asking everyone to consider the full gamut of speakers, trainers, instructors—everyone who, in their experience, had stood before two or more persons with something to say. Their choice could be a nationally known figure, a coworker, or the leader of a local scout troop. It was not necessary to remember the person's name; it was acceptable to identify the person in some other way, such as "the keynote speaker for last year's sales convention." I didn't want to place any limits on their selection. The detailed responses to my questions are summarized in the Appendix.

From the more than 1,000 responses I received, I randomly selected 200 for more detailed analysis. This review revealed a surprising number of similar perceptions that have become the cornerstone of my Speakers Training Camp. I share these findings with you, and I am confident that with this information, you can become someone's favorite speaker someday!

1. Listen to Your Audience

Get ready for the three most important things audiences like about their favorite speakers—and the three most important things you'll learn in this book. The audience responses were overwhelmingly weighted toward some simple advice to presenters.

Ranked according to number of responses, audiences say:

1. Be enthusiastic.
2. Be interesting—use humor and stories.
3. Be knowledgeable—know your stuff.

The secret to great presentations is not complicated at all. Audiences want a speaker who is outwardly excited about the topic, who uses bursts of humor, fun, and personal stories and examples to convey the message, and who is an expert in the topic.

2. Captivate With *Steak*, *Sizzle*, and *Style*

I packaged these concepts, giving them some snappy terms, and I refer to them as the three *S*'s of Spectacular Speakers (see Figure 1-2).

I categorized the survey's responses into three areas: *steak, sizzle,* and *style.*

    1. STEAK: Information, content, message, organization
    2. SIZZLE: Stories, humor, anecdotes, audience participation—things that make a presentation interesting
    3. STYLE: Gestures and voice: how a person moves, how his or her voice sounds, personality

Figure 1-2. Spectacular Speaker's triangle.
Three S's of Spectacular Speakers

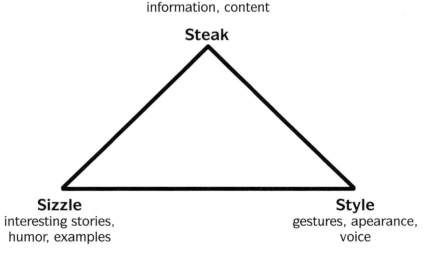

information, content
Steak

Sizzle
interesting stories,
humor, examples

Style
gestures, apearance,
voice

3. Work Harder on Your *Sizzle* and *Style*

Most respondents ranked style and sizzle above steak.

That's right. Over half of the analyzed sample gave style (gestures, voice, personality) as the most desirable quality in their favorite speaker. About one-third stressed sizzle—stories, humor, anecdotes, audience participation—as most important. Only about 17 percent saw steak—information, content, message—as most important.

4. Avoid the Ten Terrible Turn-offs

Most people, at some time, have griped about something annoying that a speaker has said or done. Sometimes they're even bored into oblivion. There is a wide variety of complaints. *Reading a presentation* is definitely a turn-off. A presentation with *no pizzazz* is hard for most to endure. The *"uh" syndrome* drives most folks batty. *Nervous habits, speaking too long*—the list is endless. But the number-1 complaint is not necessarily what you would expect. In fact, I was a little surprised to see that most of my respondents singled out, as the greatest turn-off:

MONOTONE VOICE

Perhaps the audience interprets a monotone voice as a strong signal of lack of enthusiasm. If this is true, then lots of voice fluctuations and voice energy are needed to convey enthusiasm (which the audiences have indicated is their number-1 request).

After everyone had completed the surveys, I asked the individuals in the group to explain their answers. I could tell that when we came to the section about speaker complaints, *"What is the worst thing a speaker can do to turn you off, bug you, even make you grind your teeth in agony?"* the audience was eager to share their horror stories. They could hardly wait to outdo one another in the "worst speaker I've ever seen" department. It was as though they were unleashing years of pent-up emotions.

Audiences have a strong and eager voice when it comes to complaints about speakers. Here are the *ten terrible turn-offs* (in order):

1. Monotone voice
2. Reading
3. Being boring, uninteresting
4. The "and-uh" syndrome (uh, um, you know . . .)
5. Lack of preparation: being unorganized, rambling, becoming sidetracked
6. Nervous habits: fidgeting, swaying, annoying body language
7. Speaking too long, going overtime
8. Repeating, repeating, repeating
9. Not making eye contact
10. Not relating to the audience: no audience involvement, not tuned in to the audience's needs

Besides the top ten, there are additional things that can disturb the audience. Many of them seem petty, but they can be so grating to someone sitting in the audience that he or she will stop listening to the message. What a great way to take a personal inventory on possible blunders. Remember, the audience was asked to list the *worst* thing a presenter can do. The list of audience turn-offs continues (in no particular order):

+ Arrogance
+ Going overboard on details: too many numbers on an overhead transparency, "a zillion words" on one transparency
+ Droning
+ No facial expression
+ No humor
+ Humor that doesn't work: bad jokes, discrimination, etc.
+ Not knowing the facts
+ Acting like a know-it-all
+ Inappropriate language, slang

- Talking too fast
- Mumbling
- Talking too softly
- Covering too much in a short period of time
- Grammatical errors
- No message
- Hostility
- Insecurity
- Not getting to the point
- Losing control of the audience
- Having no personality
- Being too serious
- Put-downs

5. Be Creative With Both Technical and Nontechnical Audiences

Finally, I was surprised when I compared the answers of one professional group with those of another. I had thought that engineers and lawyers, for example, would be most interested in the technical expertise of the presenters, whereas trainers and marketing professionals might lean toward more flamboyant, entertaining speakers. I was wrong! On the contrary:

All types of audiences, regardless of profession, favored creative speakers!

Whether I was analyzing a group of computer experts, accountants, or salespeople, the same pattern emerged. Approximately 85 percent of the people in any group said, "Be dynamic." "Motivate me." "Entertain me." Only about 15 percent were most interested in the bottom line, data, and facts.

Who says speaking has to be difficult? You just give the audience what they want, *steak, sizzle,* and *style,* and you avoid the terrible turn-offs.

6. Audiences Want Steak: Know Your Stuff

According to the audience members, here are the top seven things you can do to ensure that you are delivering just the right "steak." Audiences say:

- ✓ Be knowledgeable—know the topic thoroughly.
- ✓ Be organized. Use a logical and simple format. Ideas should flow easily.
- ✓ Have a clear message.
- ✓ Focus on the main issues. Get to the point.
- ✓ Make your points clear and memorable.
- ✓ Be prepared.
- ✓ Give the audience some how-to ideas.

7. Audiences Want Sizzle: Be Interesting

Sizzle is what happens when you add some heat to the "steak." It's a message zipped up with interest, creativity, and entertainment. Among ways to do this, humor was the overwhelming favorite. That was expected. But what was interesting was that all types of audiences during all types of presentations ranked humor as the number-1 item they liked in presenters. All types of audiences like humor. They rank it as their favorite speaker skill. Even when the subject was serious or technical, the audience enjoyed a good laugh. When it comes to laughter, there are no dividing lines between professions. Laughter is universal.

The following are the top eight requests for sizzle:

- ✓ Use humor. Have fun.
- ✓ Be interesting. Do something creative.
- ✓ Tell stories.
- ✓ Relate your message to the audience.
- ✓ Use audience participation.
- ✓ Relay personal anecdotes.
- ✓ Give real-life examples.
- ✓ Be entertaining.

In addition to humor, stories were also very popular with the various audiences. Listeners particularly enjoy personal stories and true-to-life experiences, especially those that relate to their world.

8. Audiences Want Style: Be Enthusiastic

Style comments cover (1) gestures and nonverbals (what we see) and (2) voice (what we hear).

For example, one attorney cited former President Kennedy as his favorite speaker for three reasons. He was:

1. "Engaging—you wanted to hear what he had to say."
2. "Sincere—you felt like he was speaking to you."
3. "Dynamic—every word seemed to count; you didn't want to turn away or miss anything."

Audiences want to see outward signs of enthusiasm in gestures and voice. Not one respondent preferred a soft-spoken, easygoing, mellow, laid-back style. Audiences are looking for outgoing personalities in their presenters.

Listed below (in order) are the eight most critical style components identified by the audiences:

1. Enthusiasm
2. Confidence
3. Dynamism
4. Sincerity
5. A strong and commanding voice
6. Passion
7. Voice fluctuations
8. An articulate presenter

Develop Your Own Steak, Sizzle, and Style

As my research developed and the concepts of steak, sizzle, and style emerged, I began using these three categories in my Speakers Training Camps. I found that the simplicity was just what my trainees wanted. Rather than bombarding them with an overwhelming amount of information, I decided to package the entire training into the three categories *steak, sizzle,* and *style*. I'd like to do the same thing for you. Keep it simple. Delivering presentations is not a monstrous task. Once you think in terms of steak, sizzle, and style, you'll see how easy it is. The chapters in this book are also organized according to those three critical areas. You'll learn ninety-three more ways to captivate a business audience.

Chapter 2

Connect With Your Audience

It takes two: you and the audience. This chapter talks about the stuff in the middle—the glue, the bond, the connection between speaker and listener. With a plan and lots of ambition, you will have a better understanding of your audience's point of view. Your audience, in turn, will be ready and willing to accept your message.

9. Know Your Audience
10. Find an Informant
11. Step Into Their Shoes
12. Get in Synch With Your Audience
13. Become an Insider
14. Activate Their "On" Buttons
15. Enhance Your Charisma Factor
16. Develop Your OOMPH
17. Reach Into Their Souls
18. Tame the Troublemakers

"My boss is great. He speaks on issues important to me and talks about things I can relate to. He seems to be talking directly to me."

Service Consultant

9. Know Your Audience

No two audiences are the same. If you do your homework, you will be prepared to design your message for a particular audience. Even if you are delivering your presentation to people you know, don't overlook these issues:

- ✓ How many people?
- ✓ What is the age range?
- ✓ Male or female?
- ✓ What are their responsibilities and job titles?
- ✓ Have they heard presenters on this topic before?
- ✓ What is their interest in your topic?
- ✓ How much do they know about your topic?
- ✓ Are they in agreement with you?
- ✓ Who are the decision-makers?
- ✓ What are their expectations?
- ✓ What are their top three concerns/needs regarding this topic?
- ✓ What are their hobbies and interests?
- ✓ Are there any current "hot buttons" at work?
- ✓ Are there any sensitive issues?
- ✓ If you are speaking in another part of the United States or another country, what special factors do you need to consider?
- ✓ Are there any community issues you should be aware of?
- ✓ What do they expect you to wear?
- ✓ What types of stories and examples would work best with this audience?

10. Find an Informant

To discover vital insider information and really be a person in the know, you have to become a sharp detective. But how do you go about it?

First you need an informant. It might be someone in the organization—your contact person. It might be someone who will be in your audience. It might be someone in the personnel department. Find someone who knows the guts of the organization. Some information might not come from a person at all. Explore the news in the community newspaper, the company newsletter, posters on the company walls, plaques, awards—anything that will help you to discover more about your audience.

Here are four discovery questions that will aid in your search:

1. What are three current and important community issues:

    a. _____

    b. _____

    c. _____

2. What are the employees facing in terms of:

    ✦ Problems _____

    ✦ Challenges _____

    ✦ Successes _____

3. What are their top two concerns regarding the topic of my presentation?

    a. _____

    b. _____

4. Are there any significant events such as strikes, relocations, mergers, top sales year, birthdays, promotions? _____

11. Step Into Their Shoes

Take your shoes off. Right here, right now—do it! Yes, that means you. It's tough to do it, isn't it? Go ahead. . . . I know, you're thinking, "Oh gee, she doesn't really mean me, does she?" Yes, I do. Take your shoes off, and imagine putting on the shoes of your listeners. By physically removing your shoes, you give yourself a physical and mental jolt. That's exactly what most presenters need when they think about the audience—a giant jolt.

Too many speakers take their message and try to cram it down the throats of their listeners without any regard for those listeners. Do not take that one-way ego trip. Instead, make a connection between your message and the individuals in your audience.

During one of his TV specials the popular country-and-western singer Garth Brooks explained how he prepares for a given audience. Long before his performance, while his team of experts is setting the stage, he hikes up to the top row in the hall and sits in the worst seat in the house. He wants to see things from that ticket holder's viewpoint. Garth imagines what he will look like on stage—a semiblur of musical magic. He knows the importance of appealing to everyone in his audience. During the performance, it was evident that he was reaching out—with his eyes, with his hands, and with his whole being—to everyone in the audience, those in the cheap seats as well as those in the front row. Many times during the performance, he would lock onto someone's eyes—especially those of the person sitting in that one very special seat. To Garth, this was his way of telling all the people in the audience that they were important.

Ask yourself the following questions about your audience. They will help you determine whether or not this audience will be receptive to your message.

- ✓ What is the mood of the people in the audience? Tired? Eager? Unresponsive?
- ✓ What will they be doing prior to your talk?
- ✓ What will they be doing after your talk?
- ✓ Are they willing or forced listeners?
- ✓ What outside influences are on their minds: weather, kids, company problems, deadlines?
- ✓ What are their expectations regarding your talk?
- ✓ Do they agree or disagree with your point of view?
- ✓ If the people in the audience put on your shoes, how would their presentation differ from the one you had planned?

Figure out the answer to the last question, then go back to the drawing board.

12. Get in Synch With Your Audience

Observe the mood of your audience, and use it to your advantage. One hot morning on the Oregon coast, I attended a conference of meeting planners. After a scavenger hunt, party, and get-acquainted session the night before, this group was already in a semirowdy and ready-to-laugh state. This was a group that convened once a year, and most of the people knew one another well. The people were also highly jovial and outspoken. The speaker was scheduled to give a three-hour session on using humor in the workplace. It was to be the highlight of the educational workshops. Instead, it turned out to be a complete bomb. The speaker didn't recognize the mood of the group and adapt to it. Instead, when the group laughed, made funny remarks, and asked questions that indirectly poked positive fun at other participants, the speaker took it as a personal attack. She turned cold and disorganized, and even changed her topic in midstream to her "ace" topic: male/female communications. She bombed again. Why? Because she wanted to be the main event. And the audience wanted to be an active, fun, jovial part of the program. The speaker was not in synch, and it made her sink!

To get in synch with your audience, you'll need to:

1. Do your homework before the session (see Tips 9, "Know Your Audience" and 10, "Find an Informant").
2. Talk to members of your audience right before the session. Get a feel for the mood.
3. Once the group has gathered, observe their vital signs. Are they paying attention? How willing are they to participate? Are they disruptive? What state are they in: serious? fun? blah? neutral? negative?
4. Adjust your behavior and your remarks to fit the goal and the audience. For example, if the goal is to discuss the serious decline in sales, and the audience comes in

with a "blah" attitude, you'll need to preface your remarks with "It's time to wake up to reality. . . ."

13. Become an Insider

An aerospace company manager faced a problem of declining morale in his department. Prior to holding a meeting to discuss the subject, he decided to spend a week working the floor with the first shift. He wanted to get a firsthand view of what the problems were. When he conducted his meeting, he spoke as an insider instead of as a "white shirt" manager. His ideas were met with rousing approval. Many of his subordinates complimented him on being able to get to the root of the problems. Becoming an insider was his ticket to success.

Several years ago I was asked to do a workshop for Nike's sales managers. I didn't have much knowledge of the athletic shoe industry, except for the pair of racewalking shoes I wore on my four-mile jaunts. I needed to explore the inner workings of the business, and so I arranged to spend a few days on the road with one of the sales reps. I learned all about crowded shoe storage nooks, too-busy buyers, hectic schedules, no-shows. I used these road stories to liven up my presentation. I could see the added alertness each time I used one of these examples. I could tell by the warm response and interaction after the program that the group really appreciated my attempts at understanding their world.

What can you do to obtain that inside angle? If you don't have time to physically take on the role, then perhaps you could interview two or three people who are insiders. Use the insiders' stories and examples in your presentation. Of course, give them credit for providing you with the information. The most important point is that you want to know as much as you can about your topic with as much credibility as possible. Getting close to the action is the best way to go.

14. Activate Their "On" Buttons

What types of subjects ignite that audience spark? First, consider the audience, then think about these possibilities:

✓ How your topic will affect their everyday lives
✓ Business
✓ Sports
✓ Money
✓ Family
✓ People
✓ Relationships
✓ News of the day
✓ News of the community
✓ News of the company
✓ Industry-related stories and examples

For example, if I am appearing before 250 business managers, 50 percent male, 50 percent female, I include as many of the above as I can. Most often, I lean more toward golf stories, family or personal stories, and industry-related material. That is part of my style—my uniqueness. I love to tell those golf stories. Golf is my passion, and an extremely important part of my life. However, there's nothing more boring to a nongolfer than golf stories. If I know that there are mainly nongolfers in the crowd, I'll tell only one or two quick golf stories with universal appeal.

Don't get stuck in a topic rut. I once attended a keynote speech delivered by a Vietnam veteran. The audience was very attentive for the first thirty minutes. His war stories were thrilling and captivating. But he lost the audience for the last half of his presentation. What had started out being interesting became commonplace—the audience needed some more variety, especially something that would relate to their present world. In order to truly connect with your audience, you need to bridge the gap between what you're saying and those to whom you're saying it. Put the topic on their laps and give them something to take with them. The audience wants both a simple, clear message and some practical how-to ideas.

15. Enhance Your Charisma Factor

My sister, Judy, is one of the most charismatic people I know. Instantly people are drawn to her. She is likable, lovable, and warm. When I ask audiences to name some charismatic speakers, names like John Kennedy, Martin Luther King Jr., and Zig Zigler are often mentioned. What makes these people so special?

Charisma is a magical quality possessed by only a few. However, you can increase your charisma factor by absorbing two important principles:

1. *People like people who really like people.*
   + Smile.
   + Use steady, direct eye contact.
   + Nod in agreement.
   + Say positive things, be enthusiastic, give compliments such as "That's good!" and "Nice job!"
   + Develop your sense of humor; lighten up!
   + Speak with energy and enthusiasm.

2. *People like people who are just like them.* Think about being at a party. You're circulating, but you feel out of place because you don't know anyone. Then you meet someone who loves trout fishing just as much as you do. Pow! The chemistry starts bubbling. You're having a good time, and chances are you like this person. You have something in common. "Common ground" is one of the sizzle ideas discussed in Chapter 4.

Besides finding common interests such as background, family, work, or hobbies, get in synch with your audience's communication patterns. Use the same terms as they do (soda vs. pop, sack vs. paper bag). Match their vocal speed and intensity. For example, the east coast has a much faster "beat" than the South or the west coast.

16. Develop Your OOMPH

Audiences like presenters with OOMPH: *O*ne *O*utstanding *M*emorable *F*eature. What makes you different? If you were a product, in what way would you stand out from the competition? Memorable speakers have a special "something" about them. They differ from the norm—in either appearance, style, voice, or message. Let's take a look at what some presenters have made their personal trademark.

GERRY SPENCE, a famous lawyer, wears a suede, fringed cowboy-type jacket. His hair is also fairly long for a lawyer. JEANNIE ROBERTSON, a humorist, is over six feet tall; she's also a former Miss North Carolina and a basketball star. Not only does Jeannie have a very striking appearance, but she jokes about her height, her beauty contest experiences, and her basketball memories. She also has a southern accent. JOSÉ EBER, a famous hairstylist, has very long hair and wears a feather on his cowboy hat. In addition, he has a charming accent. SALLY JESSE RAPHAEL, talk-show host, wears large red-rimmed glasses. What can you do to create a one-of-a-kind image?

Some presenters are famous for a particular theme. Ken Blanchard is *The One-Minute Manager*; Harvey McKay is famous for his book *Swim With the Sharks*; Wayne Pickering, professional speaker and health expert, is known as "The Mango Man." What punchy theme can you create for your next presentation?

Style is that magic combination of voice and gestures that is like a presentation fingerprint. Styles can be changed and enhanced. Johnny Carson, a fairly shy person, changed his style to outgoing and funny when he was on stage. Tom Peters also turns up the extrovert meter when he appears before a large audience. Another speaker, who had a heavy New York accent, gained in popularity when he switched from a "middle-of-the-road" to an "in-your-face" style.

17. Reach Into Their Souls

How many presenters have you heard over the years? What do you remember from what was said? If you're like most people, you don't remember much. Most presenters fade quickly from our memories. The ultimate connection for any speaker is to have some type of long-lasting effect on the audience. Here are three ways to reach into their souls:

1. *Make them think.* Wake them up. Say it in a way it's never been said before. Help them break out of neutral gear. Give them new ideas, new thoughts, or new solutions to an old issue. Keep

your message simple and memorable—one sentence that you repeat as your theme throughout your talk.

2. *Make them do.* Give them the "how to" tools to make the change. Tell them how. Tell them why. Tell them to go do it. If they're not going to change in some way after your presentation, why bother making it in the first place? Give them a pat on the back. Give them encouragement.

3. *Make them laugh.* If you can add the element of fun and laughter to your presentation, you'll experience a very special audience bond. People who laugh together develop a type of hallowed harmony, an energy that reaches way into the gut. Of the three soul-reaching elements, this is the toughest one for most people. It is worth the effort. Start your humor file today. Focus mainly on the fun and funny in your own life. Remember, too, that you can generate lots of laughter without telling a joke. Piggyback on the humorous things people say and do in your session. Poke fun at yourself; poke fun at life's little disasters.

18. Tame the Troublemakers

A critical part of maintaining the audience bond is being able to handle the group gracefully even when things aren't going your way. When it comes to handling troublemakers, be a trouble-shooter. Like John Wayne, always be prepared for the ambush. The following are four common types of troublemakers and tips on dealing with them gracefully.

1. *Motor-mouths* (two people chatting constantly). Walk toward the conversationalists, touch one of the culprits on the shoulder, and ask if he or she has a question. Another way to handle this situation is with . . . silence and direct eye contact.

2. *Bumps-on-a-log* (people who are unresponsive during audience participation). When asking a question, don't put anyone on the spot by calling his or her name. Instead, wait patiently for a volunteer. If the audience is reluctant to participate, have them write their response first, then respond orally. This will give them a chance to think, and they'll become willing partici-

pants. Ask them a question in their area of expertise. Sometimes you need to clarify or rephrase the question. If you're doing activities in small groups, it will help if you shuffle the people occasionally.

3. *Snipes* (people who are out to "snipe" you with negative comments or questions). Don't become defensive or argue with a snipe. Let the person air his or her concern. Ask the rest of the audience how they feel about the issue. Usually the audience will pounce on the snipe for you! Or, you can use a two-step escape. First, paraphrase the question or concern ("I hear what you're saying . . ."). Second, explain your point of view ("It's been my experience . . .").

4. *Scene-Stealers* (people who dominate the session with comments or questions). When the scene-stealer strikes, say, "Let's get some input from some of the other people." Physically move away from the person and withdraw eye contact. Look away. This is a powerful signal. The scene-stealer should feel as though his or her flame has just been doused. If the problem persists, talk to the person during the break. Or you can tell the person that you will be available after the session for further discussion. Sometimes I use the time-out signal to stop the action.

Chapter 3

Steak: Organization Made Easy

Keep your organization *simple.* The simpler it is, the easier it will be for both you and the audience to remember the main points. Audiences appreciate basic formats such as "The Five Pitfalls of Starting a New Business" or "Achievements and Challenges for Today's Boy Scouts." With very simple designs, it's very easy for you to organize the main facts. This chapter presents ideas for preparing your talk—simply and clearly:

19. Think Like a Kid: Jump-Start Your Presentation
20. Spin an Idea Web
21. Plan for Steak and Sizzle
22. Create a Clear Focus
23. Choose Three to Five Main Topics (the Body)
24. Jazz Up the Main Points
25. GRABM With a Great Introduction
26. Make Your Summary Memorable
27. Check the Sizzle Supply
28. Storyboard Your Ideas
29. Scoop and Deliver: Keep Your Notes Simple
30. Anchor Your Message
31. Plan for Persuasion

 "My favorite speaker . . . her ideas were clear, concise, and to the point."

—Manager, Volunteer Services

19. Think Like a Kid: Jump-Start Your Presentation

You're ready to plan the "best presentation on earth," but you have a giant case of brain drain—you simply don't know where to start. Calm down; it's easy. In five minutes, you'll have a wealth of ideas. Guaranteed! In fact, the technique we'll use was inspired by my daughter Lauren, who was eight years old at the time.

One day after school, Lauren came running up to me with great excitement. She wanted to show me a story she was writing for school. With a big grin, she showed me this piece of paper with words and scribbles and circles and lines all over it. I said, "Lauren, this doesn't look like a story." She said, "It's my story web. These are my ideas to think about when I write the story." I said, "Wow, this could help the people I work with plan their presentations."

I call it an idea web, and I've been using the concept for years in my Speakers Training Camps. It really helps people to think of ideas quickly and easily. Besides, it's actually fun!

One of my clients, John, a financial planner, said that an idea web helped to save the day for him. John's boss was scheduled to deliver a very important sales presentation with big dollars on the line when he suddenly came down with the flu. John was asked to step in. John created an idea web in five minutes, color-coded his main points, and delivered the presentation right from the web. He said that his listeners were so impressed that they asked for a crash course in idea webbing. It works. And best of all, it's quick and easy.

20. Spin an Idea Web

To get started on your presentation, you'll need a large piece of blank paper, a pen, and a timer. I think you'll be surprised at how many ideas you can generate in a very short period of time.

1. Start with a blank sheet of paper.
2. Write down the topic of your presentation in the middle of the paper, and circle it.

3. Before you start, get into a spontaneous, kidlike frame of mind. There are no rules and no boundaries. Write fast—the faster, the better. Don't let your pen stop. Make no corrections. Just write fast. Write the first thoughts that enter your mind. Try to fill up the whole page with ideas.

4. Your time commitment is five minutes. Set a timer.

5. Begin. Write down your ideas quickly, using circles, connecting lines, arrows. Use any form you like. If ideas seem to be connected, you can connect them with lines or spokes.

6. Make no judgments. Simply write whatever comes to mind. Don't worry about neatness, spelling, or quality. All you want at this stage is massive quantity.

7. Keep writing until the five-minute timer goes off. Then sit back and take a look at what you've created. Did you fill up the whole page?

8. Take a short break, and then look at the page. At this stage, usually a few key ideas will pop out at you. Identify three to five main areas that you'd like to cover in your presentation. You should start to feel a sense of direction.

9. You can use color to connect ideas or identify main topic areas.

Another option is to use a computer. Inspiration Software in Beaverton, Oregon, offers a creative ideas program called Inspiration that is very similar to the idea web. You can organize information in visual clusters with many subideas, then shift to an outline view as you develop your presentation. This program is available in both Macintosh and IBM formats.

Use idea webs any time you need to come up with some creative ideas. Let's look at a sample presentation. Imagine that you are a CEO of a large company, and you are going to make a twenty-minute presentation to kick off your new customer service training program. The first thing you need to do is follow steps one through nine and create an idea web. My web is shown in Figure 3-1. I actually set a timer for five minutes; you can see that I came up with more than fifty ideas!

Figure 3-1. Sample idea web.

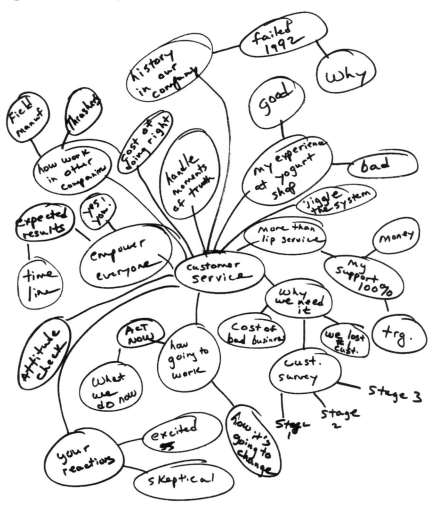

21. Plan for Steak and Sizzle

Now that you have some ideas, how can you make some sense out of them? Figure 3-2 is a presentation planner that is designed to be simple. It's based on what audiences like most: an interest-

Figure 3-2. Presentation planner.

Presentation Planner: A Steak and Sizzle Approach

Audience Focus

Objective
Message
Audience Considerations

The Presentation

Introduction
    GRABM
    WIFM
    PREVIEW
Body
    Point #1 and sub-points: steak, sizzle, steak sizzle . . .
    Point #2 and sub-points: steak, sizzle, steak sizzle . . .
    Point #3 and sub-points: steak, sizzle, steak sizzle . . .
Conclusion
    Summarize
    WIFM again!
    GRABM again!

ing message that relates to them. Let's take a closer look at the plan:

Audience Focus

Objective: I want the audience to . . .
Examples: To learn how to handle angry customers; to buy at least fifteen new computer systems; to volunteer for the hospital fun run.
Message: In one sentence, what do I want the audience to remember?
Examples: To handle angry customers, you need to empathize and agree on positive action. These computers have been rated tops by five industry magazines. The fun run

will generate $250,000 for the hospital with the help of 100 volunteers.

Audience Considerations   How can I relate this message to this audience? What are their interests in this topic?

The Presentation

INTRODUCTION

GRABM (Grab the audience's attention)

WIFM (Connect with the audience—explain what's in it for them)

PREVIEW ("Today I'm going to talk about . . .")

BODY Alternate steak and sizzle at least every six minutes. Steak is the information, content. Sizzle is the creative part: stories, humor, audience involvement, examples, props.

1. Point 1 and subpoints: steak, sizzle, steak, sizzle . . .
2. Point 2 and subpoints: steak, sizzle, steak, sizzle . . .
3. Point 3 and subpoints: steak, sizzle, steak, sizzle . . .

CONCLUSION

Summarize ("To summarize . . . ," "To wrap it up . . . ," "Before I go . . .")

WIFM again!

GRABM again!

22. Create a Clear Focus

In order to zoom in on your topic, you need three things:

1. An objective
2. A message
3. An understanding of your audience (see Chapter 2)

Do you want your presentation to inform the audience? To entertain them? To motivate them? To sell a product or idea? To gather their input? To determine your purpose, complete this sentence:

Objective: I want the audience to . . .

     Example: I want the audience to use the three key elements of knock-your-socks-off customer service.

Message: In one sentence, what do you want the audience to remember? The message is the key overriding theme of the entire presentation. It should be repeated about six times during the presentation, most importantly at the end of the talk. It is like the recurring chorus of a song. You want the audience to remember this message. It must be clear. It must be simple. It must be repeated.

    Example: Handle the moments of truth immediately.

Audience Considerations:

1. What are their interests in the topic?
2. How will they be different after hearing the presentation?
3. How can I relate the message to their needs?
4. How can they benefit from my presentation?

23. Select Three to Five Main Points (the body)

Don't start at the beginning! Start in the middle. After you have a clear focus for your presentation, develop the body of the material. Why not start with the beginning of your talk? Because trying to come up with an exciting opening is too much pressure at this stage. Instead, work on the main ideas; as you develop these topics, ideas for the opening and closing sometimes emerge automatically.

Look back over your idea web, and pick out three to five main points to form the body of your talk. You'll be surprised how these main points will pop out at you. Even a full-day presentation should have three to five main points. Remember, keep it simple. Your presentation is like a chest of drawers (see Figure 3-3). One main point is placed in each drawer. Then the drawer is filled with support material for that point: stories, facts, statistics, audience involvement exercises. The main difference between a twenty-minute talk and a two-hour one is that for the longer talk, more material is packed into each drawer.

Figure 3-3. Presentation as chest of drawers.

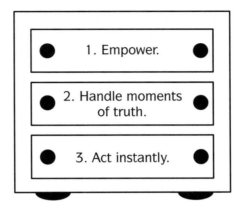

CUSTOMER SERVICE PRESENTATION
(Three main topics; put one into each drawer)

24. Jazz Up the Main Points

Take each topic and develop support material for it. You can even do a separate idea web for each topic, if you like. Be creative. Embellish the topic with the most interesting and pertinent information possible. The following examples expand the three main points in the customer service presentation.

1. *Empower:*
    + Create a trusting environment.
    + It's OK to make mistakes.
    + Ford Motor Company story.
    + I'm 100 percent behind this.
    + Don't just pay lip service to the word *empower.*
    + Four stages of empowerment.
2. *Handle moments of truth:*
    + Definition and examples.
    + Shoe store experience—what would you do?
    + What to do when a "moment of truth" occurs.
    + Solve problems.
    + Cut the bureaucracy.
3. *Act instantly:*

+ Do it right now.
+ Apologize.
+ Fix the problem, and go one step beyond.

This could be a thirty-minute talk or a two-day workshop. The degree to which each subtopic would be expanded would depend on the amount of time.

25. GRABM With a Great Introduction

The introduction of your talk has three parts: (1) GRABM, (2) WIFM, and (3) Preview.

1. *GRABM.* Grab their attention, and grab it right away. Put your energy level in high gear and:
+ Ask a question.
+ Tell a story that relates to the topic.
+ Blow them away with startling facts and statistics.
+ Use a prop.
+ Create a scenario (imagine this . . .).
+ Harness some fun (poke fun at yourself, tell a funny story).

2. *WIFM.* In a sentence or two, answer the audience's question "What's in it for me?" Tell them why they should listen; plant the benefit clearly in their minds. Some examples of effective WIFMs:
+ "I'll help you shave three years off the business learning curve."
+ "You'll come away with four great ways to manage your priorities."
+ "By the end of the day, you'll know how to conduct an effective meeting."

3. *Preview.* In one or two sentences, explain your agenda to the audience; give them a preview of what you'll be talking about. Use key phrases to focus them on the topic:
+ "Today I'll be talking about . . ."
+ "My agenda looks like this . . ."

+ "Our focus for today is . . ."
+ "My topic is . . ."

26. Make Your Summary Memorable

Here's the easy part—the summary. The summary is a flip-flop of the introduction. It has three parts: (1) summarize, (2) WIFM again, and (3) GRABM one last time.

1. *Summarize.* Let the audience know that you are winding down. Give them a cue:
+ "Before I go . . ."
+ "To summarize . . ."
+ "To wrap it up . . ."

Then, in a few sentences, present your message one last time.

2. *WIFM again.* Do the same thing you did in the introduction. Tell the audience what's in it for them. Remind them of the benefits they will experience: save time, increase income, learn a new skill.

3. *GRABM one last time.* Grab their attention again at the end of the presentation. This is your last chance to hit a homer. *Make it big!* Use the same ideas that you used in the introduction: question, story, startling facts, prop, scenario, humor, quote. Deliver them with extra oomph and conviction. Power up! If you want to add a special touch of closure to the end of your presentation, return to the theme of your opening GRABM. For example, if you started with a story about a high school buddy, you might end with a story about seeing that buddy at your last class reunion.

I have seen many speakers who have blown a few facts, forgotten some major points, and fumbled their way through their presentations. But if their summaries were clear and convincing, the audience usually forgave the presenter's blunders.

27. Check the Sizzle Supply

How do you rivet, rivet, rivet? By using sizzle, sizzle, sizzle. Chapter 4 is devoted to the art of sizzle. IN ORDER TO HOLD THE AUDIENCE'S ATTENTION, YOU MUST INSERT SOME SIZZLE EVERY SIX MINUTES. If your audience looks bored, it's generally because your talk is not interesting.

After you have completed the organization, check the sizzle supply. Be sure that at least once every six minutes, something creative is happening: a story, a prop, humor, audience involvement, an example. That's the secret to holding the audience's attention. Always ask yourself, "How could I make this point more interesting and creative?" Here are some examples:

Example 1

Boring: Discuss stages of learning—unconsciously competent, consciously competent, unconsciously incompetent, consciously incompetent.

Sizzle: Ask people in the audience to take out a piece of paper and quickly write their signatures (unconsciously competent). Then, on the next line, using the same hand, try to copy the signature exactly (consciously competent). On the next line, quickly write a signature, with the opposite hand (unconsciously incompetent). Again, using the opposite hand, write the signature as carefully as possible (consciously incompetent).

Example 2

Boring: Discuss the needs and benefits of public broadcasting.

Sizzle: Use some Bert and Ernie puppets and a four-year-old who can count to ten in Spanish (learned from watching *Sesame Street*).

28. Storyboard Your Ideas

You can visualize and perfect the flow of your presentation by storyboarding (see Figure 3-4). Movie and television producers do this as they plot out the scenes for their shows.

Figure 3-4. Storyboarding your presentation.

empower	moments of truth	act now!
Avia shoe story	define the moment	"no problem"
jiggle the system	Nordstrom tire story	Kimco Hotels

Put each single idea for your presentation on a Post-it note and organize these notes on a wall. Then, you can change and rearrange these ideas. You can use special colors for the sizzle ideas.

29. Scoop and Deliver: Keep Your Notes Simple

Your audience doesn't really care whether or not you use notes. *It's how you handle them that counts.* Glancing is OK. Reading is not. Perfect the art of scooping an idea on the page, then delivering your presentation with your eyes on the audience. Once you get the hang of this, the audience won't even know you're using notes.

Keep your notes large and simple. Your notes should have

no more than a few words on a line—merely words to trigger your thoughts. I like to put my notes on lined yellow paper. I print them with a medium black Flair pen. Each line contains only three to five words, and there is space between the lines so that they have scoopability (a thought can be scooped up quickly while you are delivering your message). You can hold your notes (staple several pages together so that they don't flap), or you can put them down on a podium or table. If you hold your notes, continue to gesture with your free arm and hand. Don't put a death-grip on your notes.

Customer Service Notes

GRABM:	Running shoes story
WIFM:	Improve customer surveys to 98th percentile
PREVIEW:	Three one-million-dollar ideas
BODY:	1. Empower:

                    ✓ Entrust decision making to all employees.

                    ✓ Jiggle the system.

             2. Moments of truth:

                    ✓ Act now!

                    ✓ Dentist example

                    ✓ Search for a quick, positive solution

(These notes would continue—large, simple, and scoopable.)

30. Anchor Your Message

How much of your presentation will the audience remember one month after the fact? If you are really terrific, they will remember only one thought and one feeling. Hint: Always give them a handout to refer to later.

A great way to plant an everlasting memory is to weave a powerful anchoring message through the course of your talk: one word, one phrase, one sentence, or one symbol that sticks forever. It's almost like an advertising symbol or slogan. Think about how many speakers you've heard. Now think about how much you remember. Not much!

Coming up with a great anchor is not an easy task. It can take days to come up with something creative, but it is worth the effort. Use this anchoring message about six times in your presentation. Here are some examples:

"It costs more to do the quality job the wrong way."
"Customers are for keeps."
"Time and people are all you have."
"The Force."
"Just say no."
"Go first."
"Wow."
"Persistence."
"Honk and encourage" (paired with geese as a symbol).
"There is no security on this earth; there is only opportunity." Douglas MacArthur (paired with Blacktip Shark as a symbol)

Other symbols might be a Hershey kiss, thumbs up, an albino horse, or blue M&M's.

31. Plan for Persuasion

So far, this chapter has focused on informative presentations. Let's take a look at persuasive presentations, in which you are trying to sell a product, service, or idea. There is one big difference between *selling* and *telling*. This difference is *asking*. The only way you can sell to someone is if you can fulfill her needs. In order to fill her needs, you must find out what those needs are. It sounds easy, but over 75 percent of sales presentations focus on assumptions, and never bother to ask the audience or buyers what they are looking for. **Find the buying trigger: What specifically is the buyer looking for?** Sometimes it's something seemingly small and insignificant. One person chose one $50,000 car because it had a holder for her coffee cup, and the other $50,000 car she was considering did not! Another person based his choice of a new computer system on the friendly repair staff. **Find the buying trigger, and you make the sale!**

Whether you are selling a product, a service, or an idea, here's a format for your strategy.

1. Open your presentation with a GRABM, WIFM, preview.
2. Ask the audience a question that will identify the buying trigger:

    "What are your top two priorities in choosing a health club?"

    "What is most important to you when looking for a vacation spot?"

    "Why are you interested in learning about sexual harassment?"

    If the audience is large, you can poll the audience beforehand or ask for a show of hands during the session.
3. Focus on key issues. Take each need which the audience has identified, and explain how your product, service, or idea fulfills this need. Remember: steak, sizzle, steak, sizzle . . .
4. Give examples for each issue. Steak, sizzle, steak, sizzle, . . .
5. Add any other pertinent details. Steak, sizzle, steak, sizzle, . . .
6. Close with a summary, WIFM, GRABM, request for action.

Part Two
Sizzle

Chapter 4

Add Sizzle Every Six Minutes

What *wows* an audience? What keeps their attention riveted, begging for more? For over ten years, I have researched those questions. Using the **Memorable Speaker Survey**, I have recorded responses from all types of audiences, including lawyers, secretaries, financial experts, trainers, and hundreds more. I was amazed to find that the things that captivate one group are the same things that captivate the other groups. There are no differences in the preferences of these diverse groups. However, within any given audience, a pattern does occur. Approximately 85 percent of the people in any audience prefer speakers who use techniques such as humor, creativity, motivation, audience involvement, and stories to convey their message. The remaining 15 percent prefer the "meat and potatoes" approach—without garnish. They prefer speakers who zero in on the bottom line, data, and facts.

What can you do to become a memorable speaker? Use the steak and sizzle approach to capture both groups. Present pertinent information (steak), then alternate with something interesting, such as a story or the use of a prop (sizzle). In order to keep your audience at the peak of attention, add sizzle once every six minutes.

In this chapter, you will learn ten different ways to add sizzle to your talk and heighten your audience's attention. REMEMBER: EVERY SIX MINUTES!

    32. Use Stories and Examples
    33. Quote an Interesting or Unusual Authority

34. Show-and-Tell (Demonstrate a Product or Idea)
35. Find Common Ground With Your Audience
36. Dazzle Them With Props
37. Use Strategic Name Dropping
38. Self-Disclose (the Whoops Factor)
39. Showcase Your Hobby
40. Activate Your Audience: Involve Them
41. Make Them Laugh

"I had a college professor who incorporated props and gimmicks in creative ways to illustrate what he was teaching."

—Marketing Analyst

---

32. Use Stories and Examples

When presenters tell me that some talks are so technical that there's no room for anything interesting, I give them the "sizzle challenge." I challenge these speakers to find the dry spots, and then jazz up the message by using a very simple phrase: "for example . . ."

When a speaker uses a story or example, you can see an instant change come over the audience. Eyes look up, doodling stops; they become still and quiet. When you add some sizzle, it's like turning on light bulbs in the minds of the listeners. The more often you turn on the switch (use sizzle), the higher the attention level.

Personal stories work best. Fill your stories with vivid descriptions, real locations, and people's names. Give them lots of color and life. Instead of saying, "The other day I walked into a computer store, and the salesman was so fantastic that I bought two new systems," say this: "Friday I went over to Tri-Star Computer in Arlington and within fifteen seconds a salesperson named Gordy handed me a cup of cappuccino and a maple bar. Within two minutes, he'd asked all the right questions and was showing me the model I needed. Twenty-five minutes later I was out the door with two new PS 420's and an appointment for an in-office set-up and demo."

Along with personal stories, think about using news items or stories borrowed from resource materials. Two of my favorite sources are *USA Today* and The *Wall Street Journal*. BUT, BEWARE OF THE OVERUSED STORY. Your material needs to be original and rarely used by others.

33. Quote an Interesting or Unusual Authority

Get the maximum mileage from someone else's words. How? First, use only quotations that really excite you at the gut level. If you don't "feel" the message, it will come across as matter-of-fact. You need to burn those words into the hearts of your audience. Deliver the quotation with extra oomph: voice energy, direct eye contact, meaningful pauses, emphatic gestures. If you need to read the quotation, be sure to maintain eye contact with the audience as much as you can.

Choose something unique. The best quotations don't always come from famous people. How about your Aunt Martha or the Little League coach? You can use quotations from books, the morning paper, your tennis pro. One very successful speaker, a 6'10" powerful executive, often anchors his message with phrases such as "My grammy always told me . . ." or "Grammy had three things to say about failure . . ." The contrast of the successful executive quoting words from his grammy adds lots of interest to his presentations. My favorite source for quotations is *The Executive Speechwriter Newsletter*, published by Words, Inc., in St. Johnsbury, Vermont.

If a quotation falls flat, it's usually because the delivery was dull and lifeless, or the quotation has been heard too many times before. Don't let this happen to you. Use a maximum of three quotations in your talk. Remember, you want to be the expert. Overreliance on quotations takes the emphasis away from *you*.

34. Show-and-Tell (Demonstrate a Product or Idea)

Julie turned shades of green and purple during her first presentation. She could barely breathe, and elephant tears were welling in her eyes. For the first time in the history of the Speakers Training Camp, I thought I might lose a participant. Until . . . she discovered the magic of demonstration.

Julie was a hairstylist who wanted to demonstrate beauty products nationwide for a very large company. Before her next presentation, I encouraged her to bring in some hair sprays and goop and gel. She could do a demo on me for her next talk. It worked! Julie was in her element—she talked while working with my hair. The activity relieved her from feeling that all the attention was focused on her presentation skills. Instead, attention was focused on her demonstration. The audience was glued to every word. She did a great job, and I ended up with a super hairstyle.

Demonstrations are guaranteed crowd-pleasers. They are the "show" factor of show-and-tell. Here are just a few examples that can enliven a presentation:

+ Demonstrate how the new color printer works—show them the results.
+ Play the role of the scatterbrained supervisor.
+ Use the voice of an impolite telemarketer.
+ Show the mechanics of a good putting stroke.
+ Demonstrate various etiquette aspects of dealing with Japanese executives.

To catch and hold the audience's attention, don't just tell, show-and-tell!

35. Find Common Ground With Your Audience

My ultimate speaking challenge came when I had to face 750 butchers. I was preparing a customer service workshop for a butchers' convention. My main concern was credibility. I knew a lot about customer service, but very little about butchering. It was obvious that I needed to find some common ground—a connection to my audience.

Luckily, my Aunt Grace had been a country butcher in rural Pennsylvania. She died many years ago, but I remember that she was quite a character. Aunt Grace drove her truck from door to door and sold meat right out of the truck. She joked with her customers and treated them royally. Occasionally she would pull pranks like delivering gourmet guts instead of a porterhouse steak.

During the workshop, I sprinkled down-home Aunt Grace stories throughout my "Fifty Ways to Delight Your Customers" talk. Afterwards, many people from the audience came forward to meet me personally and to talk about Aunt Grace. My presentation would not have been as rousing if it had not had those common-ground stories. Aunt Grace was my link to the audience.

Always ask yourself, "What do I have in common with the audience?" Golf? Children? Career? Travel? Favorite football team? Love of nature? If the answer is "nothing," then go find some common ground.

One of my clients, a battalion chief for the Phoenix Fire Department, was discussing the possibility of providing a Speakers Training Camp for other chiefs and trainers within the department. He recommended that I spend a day riding on a fire truck with the firefighters so I could learn about their responsibilities and brushes with danger. What an exciting way to develop some common ground!

Suppose that you were giving a presentation to people in the automotive industry. In order to develop a bond with the audience, consider getting some firsthand experience in their world: Spend a few hours in a new car showroom or in the service garage. If that's not possible, talk to people in that industry about their experiences, joys, problems, insights. Read articles on the subject. You'll find a wealth of stories and examples, and the audience will appreciate your efforts.

36. Dazzle Them With Props

Bring out a prop and watch your audience's eyes light up. At the beginning of a speech about the benefits of chemical sprays, a Dow Chemical executive held out a big shiny red apple and said, "How would you like to have the worm back in your apple?" . . . long pause . . . His audience was motionless—captivated. The attention level was 150 percent.

That's one speech I'll always remember. The Dow executive really made an impression. He left me with a thought that I'll never forget. That's what I call "making a dent." Not only was I paying attention for the moment, but that moment was so meaningful that it became permanent. That's the ultimate mission of a presenter: to plant an idea that sticks. This speaker used both a prop and a powerful question to create the lasting effect.

Props will bring fun and increased attention to your presentations, too. The possibilities and uses are endless. Look around your house, your office, your garage, your kids' toy chest. Be creative. Here are some unique ideas:

- ✦ Hats to represent various personalities
- ✦ A broken golf club used as a pointer
- ✦ Play money
- ✦ A tape measure—snip it into pieces to make a point
- ✦ A phone to demonstrate proper telephone techniques
- ✦ Hammer, screwdriver, pliers, etc., to show how to handle negativity
- ✦ Boxes of food to make a point about advertising
- ✦ Costumes/masks (I use Darth Vader to portray the evil force of nervousness)

37. Use Strategic Name Dropping

Dropping names strategically can increase your audience's attention level in a split second. Use the names of well-known persons, places, and things.

One corporate marketing executive was losing his audience until he mentioned Jimmy Hoffa. He mentioned that he had met

Hoffa one evening at dinner in an uptown restaurant. Noticing the instant rise in attention, the executive embellished the remainder of his talk with Hoffa bits sprinkled into the message. What a boost it gave to his otherwise feeble presentation!

Name dropping can also be very effective in persuasive presentations. If you're trying to obtain a new client, mention the names of familiar and impressive companies that have already used your product or services. What potential client wouldn't be impressed if he or she knew that you were working with Procter & Gamble, NASA, and RCA?

Warning: BEWARE OF NAME-DROPPING ABUSE. Too much name dropping can be a disaster. Use this technique, but don't abuse it. A few months ago I heard a speaker who constantly referred to her training sessions in London, Paris, Australia. She did it so much that it seemed to be fueled by her ego. She was losing sight of her training objectives: to teach, not to impress the group with her foreign adventures. It's a judgment call. The reference should be intertwined with the message.

Other categories of names to drop in your presentations: sports figures, cartoon characters, famous celebrities, political figures, folk heroes, TV and movie stars, people involved in special events (the Super Bowl) or current events (items of interest in the news).

38. Self-Disclose (the Whoops Factor)

Be real. Be human. Sometimes be vulnerable. Members of your audience will empathize. Several years ago, I heard Ken Blanchard speak. He's the author of *The One-Minute Manager*. During the course of his presentation, he revealed many things about himself. He often struggled with losing weight (me, too!). He has a very messy desk (me, too!). He's been greatly challenged by the monumental role of parenthood (me, too!). Any time someone in the audience experiences a "me, too," it helps to solidify his or her bond with the speaker.

These revelations make the audience feel, "This guy is for real, he's honest and down to earth, and I believe what he says."

Once I was to deliver a presentation skills workshop to a

telecommunications company. The company's vice president did the introductions. He welcomed the participants and told them how scared he had been in his high school public speaking class. But now, after many years of experience and tons of sweat, he actually looks forward to speaking.

Here's the beauty of that self-disclosure: The message translated directly to the audience. They were probably thinking, "me, too": "I'm nervous, too; but with some work, perhaps I can become an accomplished speaker like this man."

39. Showcase Your Hobby

My hairstylist snipped and combed as she told me about the best speaker she'd ever heard. It was at a hairstyling show. The featured speaker was an expert in client communications. When I asked why she was so excited by this particular speaker, she said that he came out on stage wearing tennis clothes, holding a tennis racket, and bouncing a tennis ball. The guy was a passionate tennis player. He wove his message around some key principles in playing tennis:

1. Keep your eye on the ball (focus on the client).
2. You can win only when you serve (so serve your best every time).
3. Adapt your game to the person across the net (every client is different).

His tennis-inspired presentation was a unique and rousing success.

What hobby do you have that you might use effectively in a presentation? There are many possibilities. Here are a few:

+ Playing a musical instrument
+ Poetry
+ Photography (sprinkle some of your favorite slides into your slide show)
+ Juggling
+ Magic tricks

+ Cooking
+ A sport
+ An interesting or unusual collection

If you incorporate a hobby into your presentation, your audience not only will be entertained, but will have fun learning a little bit more about you. Let your personality soar!

40. Activate Your Audience: Involve Them

Most audiences already know 90 percent of your subject matter, even before you utter your first syllable. So, why not unleash their expertise and captivate their attention through audience involvement techniques?

First, three general guidelines:

1. It doesn't matter how many people are in the audience; involvement can be adapted.
2. Be willing to take yourself out of the limelight. Focus on the audience's issues, not yours.
3. It takes a little more time to use audience involvement than to give a straight lecture, but the increased attention and retention factors are worth it!

Now, for some activity ideas:

+ Questions/silent response (audience raises hands)
+ Audience-initiated questions
+ Building your agenda with the audience (and following it!)
+ Discussion (whole or small group)
+ Brainstorming
+ Written activity
+ Problem solving—case study
+ Contest
+ Game
+ Physical activity—practice the skills
+ Learning journals—skill diaries

+ Field trip
+ Panel
+ Debate

41. Make Them Laugh

I was six years into my speaking and training career when I realized that I had a serious problem. I had not provoked a laugh, a giggle, or even a chuckle from an audience during the entire six years! I sent myself on a mission: to become a funnier person. Through my investigation of what audiences find amusing, and through personal trial and error, I have developed the **"Boring Person's Guidelines to Humor."** They follow:

✓ Believe that you are delightfully funny, and you will become funnier.
✓ Have fun with human error. Pay attention to what's going on around you.
✓ Your life has more funny material than any joke book. Find it!
✓ Find a humor role model.
✓ Look for material everywhere: magazines, newspapers, books, TV, radio, funny stories, jokes, bumper stickers.
✓ Keep a humor file. If you don't capture humorous material, you will forget it. Write it down, clip it, snip it, save it!
✓ Personalize all humor to fit your own style and the needs of the audience.
✓ Test-drive your humor with friends, coworkers, spouse, children.
✓ If the humor passes the test drive, try it out on an audience.
✓ Keep it tasteful. **If in doubt, *don't use it!***
✓ Use material that really makes you sparkle. Deliver it with "fizz."
✓ Evaluate the audience's reaction. Then keep it, revise it, or toss it out.

Part Three
Style

Chapter 5

Control Nervousness: The *Star Wars* Theory

"I feel like a brainless, perspiring, quivering weakling who's on the verge of throwing up. That's how I feel before giving a presentation." Those are the words of a vice president of a very successful *Fortune* 500 company. Somewhere between the fun of "show-and-tell" in kindergarten and the "tell-and-sell" of corporate America, businesspeople have learned to despise speaking before a group. In this chapter, we'll look at ways to tackle "presentation panic."

42. Never Say "Nervous"
43. Think Positive Thoughts
44. Behave Like a Duck
45. Soothe Your Symptoms
46. Relax
47. Prepare! Prepare! Prepare!
48. Focus on the Audience—Not on Yourself
49. Don't Panic
50. Eat Like an Athlete
51. Exercise

I like a speaker with a "relaxed, positive style."

—Senior Assistant Counsel

42. Never Say "Nervous"

Never again say "nervous." Instead, use a new term. Call that feeling "the Force." Remember the movie *Star Wars*? There were two sides to "the Force," the dark side and the good side. The same thing is true of prespeech tension. You can think about it as a nasty prelude to failure, or you can think about it as a surge of electricity that will make you glow.

Compare a presenter's anxiety and an athlete's adrenaline. The symptoms are basically the same: racing heart, sweaty palms, knot in the stomach. The main difference is in the mental interpretation. When a person feels nervous, the feeling is interpreted as negative. However, when a person feels the flow of adrenaline, the feeling is interpreted as positive, race-horse-like energy. Imagine an Olympic ski jumper at the top of the chute waiting to bolt down the ramp. The skier probably has many feelings running through him or her. Above all, there is the positive thrust of adrenaline. That feeling is absolutely necessary for maximum performance.

The same thing is true of speaking. The jittery feelings will not, and should not, go away. Just as an athlete needs that electrified feeling, so does a speaker. Never say "nervous." Instead in the words of Obie Wan Kenobe, "May the Force be with you." You need it.

43. Think Positive Thoughts

What do you say to yourself when you're thinking about that next presentation? Are you saying, "Why me? This isn't interesting. I hate giving presentations"? Or are you saying, "I can't wait. The audience will love this. I really enjoy speaking"? Your comfort level depends on that little voice inside your head. The secret is to consciously control the dialogue. Even if you've been speaking for fifteen years, negative thoughts will still try to dominate. The voice in your head is like a record. But you are the one who chooses which side of that record to play: the positive side or the negative side.

Speaking is such a traumatic event for some of my clients

that I actually have them write some positive thoughts on an index card. Then, for an entire month prior to the presentation, they repeat the thoughts several times each day, like a continuous loop on a tape recorder. The idea is to make the positive thoughts automatic. These thoughts should be as simple as "I love to speak. My audience will enjoy my presentation. I am well prepared."

Besides thinking positive thoughts, visualize a positive speaking situation in vivid detail. See yourself wearing your best presentation attire. You look great; you glow, and you walk around the room with ease. You're smiling; the audience is alert and responsive; they're smiling, too. You say something funny, and they laugh and applaud. . . .

For each presentation, think positive thoughts and imagine a successful experience. It won't be automatic. You need to mentally orchestrate your desired outcome. Program yourself for success.

44. Behave Like a Duck

That's right. Behave like a duck: Stay calm on the surface, but paddle like crazy underneath. What's the secret of looking comfortable even when you're not? Do what the pros do. Fake it! And learn the behaviors of "calm."

- ✓ Smile a lot.
- ✓ Don't hurry. Take your time.
- ✓ Never hold anything that shows you have "the shakes" (notes that quiver, pens that vibrate, pointers that look like they're drunk).
- ✓ Act like you know what you're doing.
- ✓ Never admit that you don't know what you're doing.
- ✓ Imagine that you're giving the talk to a group of friends gathered in your living room—keep it conversational.
- ✓ Be yourself.
- ✓ Commit to having a good time.
- ✓ Breathe!

Remember this: If you do not draw attention to them, the audience will not care about most mistakes. I have seen presenters trip on stage, lose their places, stumble over words, forget main points, lose the sound on their microphones, and have to abandon faulty A-V equipment—all without any negative audience response. Next time this happens to you, handle the problem gracefully. Look cool and confident. Behave like a duck!

45. Soothe Your Symptoms

Make a list of your nervous symptoms. For most of them, there is a way to lessen the problem. Attack your symptoms rather than letting them attack you.

DRY MOUTH:	Have a pitcher of room-temperature water available.
OUT OF BREATH:	Practice deep breathing.
KNOT IN STOMACH:	Avoid caffeine and eating large meals. Get some exercise, even if it's just walking down the hallway.
POUNDING HEART:	Listen to music, exercise, practice deep breathing.
MIND GOES BLANK:	Prepare easy-to-read notes, use simple and effective audiovisuals; have the opening well rehearsed; turn it over to the audience for questions.
HOARSE VOICE:	Drink lemon juice, hot tea, or decaffeinated coffee.
TENSE VOICE:	Try voice exercises. Sing "ah" slowly up and down the scale as though you were an opera singer preparing. Make deep breathing a habit.
FACIAL TENSION:	Make exaggerated monster, clown, and goofy faces.

46. Relax

If you think about trying to relax five minutes before your presentation, it's too late. Then it's like trying to put out a burning building with a bucket of water. Prespeech relaxation works best if you start first thing in the morning, then work at it right up until the time that you speak. Here are some specific things you can do:

+ *Breathe deeply.* Breathe in through your nose for a slow count of eight, then breathe out through your mouth for a slow count of eight. Keep doing this for at least ten minutes. Use deep breathing throughout the day—make it an ongoing habit any time you feel stress.
+ *Visualize a favorite place.* Picture the details: the crashing surf, the seagulls squawking overhead, or the way the moss hangs from the trees at the edge of the trail. Keep your thoughts and visions flowing for at least ten minutes. Include the deep breathing exercise.
+ *Be your own psychologist.* For five minutes, write down your feelings in great detail. Take a short break, then look at what you've written. Imagine that you are a caring and insightful counselor. Give yourself some good advice.
+ *Listen to music.* It will synchronize your internal body rhythm (breathing and heart rate) to its own beat. Choose a lively piece when you want to be motivational and entertaining. Choose something mellow when you are leading a meeting.

47. Prepare! Prepare! Prepare!

Here's a presentation preparation checklist:

✓ Know your audience.
✓ Use easy-to-read notes with large print. Write down key ideas only. Do not write out your presentation word for word. Practice using your notes.

✓ Rehearse your talk six times. Record it on video- or audio-tape if possible.
✓ Practice using your visual aids.
✓ Have the first three minutes of your talk down cold. No notes.
✓ Know how to expand or shrink your talk as time requires.
✓ Write down the twenty questions the audience is most likely to ask. Think about your answers.
✓ Make a checklist of supplies and materials you'll be using: markers, transparencies, handouts, props, name tags.
✓ Have written directions to the meeting site.
✓ Get plenty of rest.
✓ Carry vital notes with you. Do not put them in airlines' checked baggage.
✓ Arrive at the presentation site at least one hour early.
✓ Check and test all equipment, lighting, microphone, etc.

48. Focus on the Audience—Not on Yourself

One day I walked up to a marketing specialist who was about to give his first presentation, and I asked him what was going through his mind. He said, "I want everything to be perfect. I'm thinking about not forgetting any information. I'm wondering if I'll look nervous. I hate giving presentations."

A few weeks later, I walked up to a veteran speaker, and I asked the same question. He said, "I'm thinking about the audience. I know they'll learn some things here today that they'll keep with them for the rest of their lives. I think they'll enjoy this talk, and I'm looking forward to it.

The difference? Speaker 1 was inwardly focused, concentrating on his own shortcomings. Speaker 2, on the other hand, was outwardly focused. He was thinking about the audience and the benefits they would receive from his talk.

If you have difficulty being audience-focused, write down two or three ways in which your listeners will be better off after hearing your presentation. Always have at least fifteen minutes to spare prior to your starting time. Then you'll be able to shake people's hands and mingle before you begin. This will give you some friendly faces in the crowd. It will help you to think of "them" instead of "me."

An association executive came up to me one day after a lunch speech I had given. He couldn't wait to tell me about his favorite speaker. This speaker spent at least twenty minutes shaking hands and meeting people prior to his talk. The format of his presentation was then determined by the audience: They asked questions, and he responded to their concerns. The entire group was amazed when the speaker addressed each person in the group of forty-five by his or her first name. This popular speaker was completely audience-focused.

49. Don't Panic!

Here are the most common causes of presentation panic—and their cures:

✦ *Losing your place.* Use easy-to-follow notes, with only three or four words on a line. Prewritten audiovisuals will help the flow of ideas. Take a break. Consider audience involvement.

✦ *Too much material.* Zoom in on your primary message. Make it crystal clear, and condense your thoughts into a few main points. DO NOT GO OVERTIME.

✦ *Too little material.* End early (people rarely complain about ending early). Or involve the audience in an activity or discussion.

✦ *Someone in the audience is falling asleep.* Use the 95 percent rule. If 95 percent of the people look alert and interested, don't worry. However, if quite a few people look drowsy, do something: change gears, take a break, check the room temperature, liven things up with a group activity, add more excitement to your voice and gestures.

✦ *Saying something you regret.* Use a comeback such as, "Oops! Let me press the delete button on that one!"

✦ *A-V equipment fails.* **Always have a backup plan.** If the backup plan fails, take a break. Try to remedy the problem.

Don't be afraid to ask for assistance from someone in the audience. If the equipment cannot be fixed, explain the situation to the audience, and then proceed full speed ahead. Apologize only once, then proceed!

50. Eat Like an Athlete

I never really paid much attention to what I ate before giving a presentation until one morning when my stomach felt as if it were going to erupt. It happened during a critique session for my Applause! Speakers Training Camp—one of my favorite parts of the program. After retracing my actions that morning, I tied the gut-wrenching feeling to the thick, dark (almost chewy) coffee I had been drinking. Since that time, I have done lots of personal research on what foods help and hinder presentation performance.

Here's what I've discovered: Eat like an athlete. Eat healthy foods, with plenty of protein and Vitamin C (fruits and vegetables), and avoid spicy choices. For two days prior to the presentation and for the day(s) of your presentation, eliminate caffeine and alcohol, and eat pasta (athletes call this carbohydrate-loading). Eating pasta helps to maintain energy and works wonders in overcoming jet lag. Keep your throat lubricated by drinking hot liquids (remember, no caffeine) and lots of water (room temperature is best). Stay away from milk products; they promote mucous secretions in the throat. Also, avoid medications that cause side effects such as drowsiness, light-headedness, excitability, or dry mouth.

If your presentation is lengthy, take something to munch on, such as a bagel. I find that after about two hours my stomach starts to rumble, and the only way to stop it is by having a bite to eat.

51. Exercise

I am an exercise freak. I've exercised regularly for the last twenty years. But I always thought that I was too busy on the days of my presentations to bother with it.

Until the morning I was going to deliver a presentation to about forty-five people who knew me. Their expectations were extremely high, and I wanted to knock 'em dead! I woke up that morning with a bad case of the jitters—pounding heart and out of breath. I decided to take the time to racewalk two miles. By the end of my journey, I felt exhilarated, relaxed, and confident. I was mentally and physically ready for that presentation. I even received an added bonus: a rosy, glowing, healthy-looking complexion!

One friend of mine, a traveling executive, jogs in place for twenty minutes while she watches TV in her hotel room. Another walks two miles to and from the office. Regardless of your choice of aerobic exercise, the physical and mental rewards will greatly reduce your level of stress. Find some activities that you can do even while traveling. Always pack a swimming suit, exercise clothes, and a comfortable pair of walking shoes. Remember, breathing and heart rate are keys to relaxation. Steady aerobic exercise will be your ally.

There are other hidden benefits of exercise. As an avid race-walker and golfer (I never use a cart), I often depend on exercise to enhance my creativity. If I'm looking for some great ideas to use in a presentation, I'll put the task on autopilot. About thirty minutes into the activity, the ideas surge. Researchers call it the release of endorphins. I call it "aerobic ahas!"

Chapter 6
Style: Becoming a "10"

YOU ARE THE MOST IMPORTANT FACTOR IN YOUR PRESENTATION. It is not the multimedia computer program, the nine-screen slide show, or the $60,000 video. *It is you.* This chapter will help you to develop a winning style. Since image is based on perception, you will learn what it takes to become a "10" in the eyes of the audience.

52. Remember that *You* Are Number 1 With the Audience
53. Look Like a "10"—for Men
54. Look Like a "10"—for Women
55. Communicate Eyeball to Eyeball
56. Take Up Space
57. Don't Get Stuck
58. Avoid Fiddling, Fidgeting, and Flagrant Fouls
59. Show Your Glow (Smile!)
60. Stretch Your Style
61. Evaluate Your Style

> *"My favorite speaker is Edward Shevarnadze. I liked the way he carried himself across the stage, using his body, arm and hand gestures to stress points. He made eye contact with almost everyone in the audience."*
>
> —Marketing Information Specialist

52. Remember That *You* Are Number 1 With the Audience

I once listened to a presenter who had the ultimate in high-tech computerized graphics. He could produce all sorts of tricks on the screen—fades, progressive bullets, sounds and horns to announce a new topic. He could even pipe in 350 different theme songs while his fingers danced on the elaborate keyboard. His razzle-dazzle show didn't skip a technological beat. He really knew what he was doing. There was only one problem: The customer did not buy the product he was selling.

Why? The audience was mesmerized by the computer show, but the presenter forgot one vital component: himself. People buy people. People buy people they like. The presenter did not develop any kind of relationship with his audience. They were unresponsive to him, to his ideas, and to his product. He didn't realize that the presenter is number 1 with the audience. Nothing can take the place of the personal relationship.

Another presenter was delivering the keynote address at a convention. There were approximately 750 people in his audience. One hour prior to the program, the speaker was in the room waiting for the first person to arrive. He stood at the doorway and greeted everyone personally. He shook their hands and chatted with them briefly. During his presentation, he often referred, by name, to members of his audience. He would also include tidbits that he had learned about them: "Joe Blonsky, the production manager at the East Peoria plant, told me . . . , Mary Charles had an interesting experience last night at Chez Parfait . . . , Ted Morris explained that the biggest thing in his life is that new baby due next week. . . ." The audience was in awe. This presenter had a special talent for remembering names and minute details. By personalizing the talk, he won the audience, and the business. He was number 1 with them.

53. Look Like a "10"—for Men

You are the number 1 visual in your presentation. Your appearance is extremely important.

Audience Considerations: Think about your audience. Match their values in appearance. Then dress one step above that level. Also, ask this question: "What would the audience expect me to wear?"

Business Casual: In many companies casual business attire is the norm. Look at how top management dresses, and use that as a guideline. Even when a pair of slacks and denim shirt is the norm, wear your very best on the day of the presentation. You can still be outstanding in terms of color and quality.

Colors: Choose colors that make you look good. Pay attention to the research on "power colors." Best bets: gray or navy suits for maximum confidence. Black is very formal. Choose cotton shirts in light blue or white.

To create a professional, yet friendlier impression, choose a sports jacket in place of a suit. Also, tweeds and herringbones are good here. Brown tones are acceptable (but not as striking).

The darker your skin, the more important it is that you have a light color near your face. If you compare two black men, one wearing a burgundy shirt and the other wearing a light blue shirt, the one with the light blue shirt will show up better. His face tones will be complemented by the light blue color.

Ties: Wear a conservative tie with a dash of red in it. This will make your face stand out.

Quality: Buy the best quality you can afford. It shows. Have your clothes tailored.

Shoes: Choose conservative styles, and see that they are polished. Avoid trendy and casual shoes (such as penny loafers).

Jewelry: Wear conservative rings on ring fingers only. A watch, tie bar, and lapel pin are also in good taste.

Glasses: People who wear glasses are perceived as intelligent. Keep glasses fairly conservative. Be sure they fit the size of your face. They should be larger rather than the tiny round wire-frame look. Medium tones such as tortoiseshell are good. Some darker wire frames are fine. If you have a problem with appearing unfriendly, take your glasses off occasionally. If you have a problem with inexperience or looking too young for the job, wear your glasses. However, it is difficult for the audience to see your eyes when you wear glasses—it decreases the effectiveness of your eye contact. Therefore, if contact lenses are an option for you, give them a try (but only if you can wear them comfortably without constant blinking).

Hair: Match that of your audience. Short, conservative styles are dependable.

People with beards and mustaches are often perceived as lacking in credibility. If you choose to wear a beard or mustache, be sure to keep it neat and trimmed. Being clean-shaven is the safest bet.

Fingernails: Keep them short and clean.

Role Model: Choose someone whose style and level of success you admire. Then pattern your clothing choices after theirs. My choices in the male category are Tom Brokaw and Stone Phillips, the NBC commentators, for the full-blown professional look, and Bill Cosby (great sweaters) for the casual, more relaxed look.

54. Look Like a "10"—for Women

You are the number 1 visual in your presentation. Your appearance is extremely important.

Audience Considerations: Think about your audience. Match their values in appearance. Then dress one step above that level. Also ask this question, "What would the audience expect me to wear?"

Business Casual: The trend in business dressing is becoming more casual. Always choose clothes that flatter you in terms of style and color. Jackets, even casual ones, will usually enhance your look. Take your cues from the management in your company. How do they dress? Remember to draw attention to your face through accessories and makeup. For presentation purposes always err on the side of caution.

Colors: Choose colors that make you look good. Pay attention to the research on "power colors." Best bets: Suits of medium blue, navy, gray, white, or some shades of rose/red/ burgundy. These colors work for most skin tones. Avoid pastels when you need to look powerful. For blouses, choose solid colors such as white and light blue. Avoid pronounced patterns, or florals.

A suit gives you maximum credibility. There are many style choices in suits, ranging form conservative to designer looks. Choose a style that makes you look good. Short jackets look fine on thin people; longer jackets are very flattering. I recommend designer suits in the standard power colors, such as navy, black, and burgundy. That way you can express your uniqueness and still look confident. Avoid sexy looks, such as slits, flairs, and short hemlines. Pantsuits are acceptable for less formal situations. If men in the audience are wearing suits, you'll need to wear one. The best dress will never equal a suit in terms of power.

Quality: Buy the best quality you can afford. It shows. Choose wools, wool blends, gabardines, silks, and cotton blends. Buy wrinkle-free fabrics. Have your clothes tailored.

Skirt Length: Make it between two inches above the knee and two inches below the knee.

Contrast: Think about the size of your audience. The larger the audience, the more contrast you will need in color and accessories so that attention is drawn to your face. Use maximum contrast in color between jacket and blouse (such as a French blue suit and a white blouse), then add jewelry that will stand out (such as a bold gold necklace and large earrings).

Jewelry: Wear a large gold, silver, or pearl necklace. Again, the larger the size of the group, the larger the detail. Do not wear mid-chest necklaces. That's not where you want the attention. Silk scarves, pocket scarves, and large pins work well. Earrings should be the size of a quarter or larger. Avoid dangling styles. Wear conservative rings on ring fingers only.

Shoes: Choose conservative styles, with closed toe and closed heel and no decorations, and see that they are polished. Avoid trends. Heels should be approximately two inches. Comfort is important.

Glasses: People who wear glasses are perceived as intelligent. Keep them fairly conservative. They should be larger rather than the tiny round wire-frame look. Medium tones such as tortoiseshell are good. Some darker wire frames are fine. If you have a problem with appearing unfriendly, take your glasses off occasionally. If you have a problem with inexperience or looking too young for the job, wear your glasses. However, it is difficult for the audience to see your eyes when you wear glasses—it decreases the effectiveness of your eye contact. Therefore, if contact lenses are an option for you, give them a try (but only if you wear them comfortably without constant blinking).

Hair: Shorter hair—above the shoulder increases the appearance of credibility. Straight or slightly wavy hair looks more confident than curls. Choose a style that is flattering. Also, choose one that does not get in the way while you are speaking (such as side bangs that constantly droop over your eyes). Long hair worn in upswept styles is very attractive. Hair should be a natural-looking color. Avoid bleached blond and streaked looks.

Fingernails: Keep them clean and neat, and no longer than medium length. Nail polish should be subtle.

Makeup: Yes! Wear makeup. It should be natural-looking. Again, with a larger audience, you'll need more makeup. Blush, lipstick, mascara, and earth-tone eye shadows will enhance your appearance. Avoid bright-colored eye shadows.

Role Model: Choose a clothing role model. Mine is Connie Chung, the TV newscaster. Her style is ultra-professional, with a designer influence. When I shop for presentation attire, I look into the mirror, and ask myself the question, "Is this something Connie Chung would wear?" If the answer is yes, I buy it!

55. Communicate Eyeball to Eyeball

Several years ago I went to see a presentation by Tom Hopkins, the famous sales trainer. The room was packed, wall to wall, with 1,500 people. I'll never forget how Tom—from forty rows away—made me feel as though he were speaking directly to me. He looked me right in the eyes many times. His eyes made a direct, steady connection.

Eyeball-to-eyeball eye contact was Tom's secret. You can use it, too, once you learn the trick. Look into the eyes of one individual for a steady three to five seconds. Think of carrying on an individual mini-conversation with that person. Then look at another person for three to five seconds, finish your thought, and move on to another. You'll actually sense that their eyes are responding to yours. Distribute your eye contact smoothly and deliberately in various areas of the room. Really *see* the people. Let your eyes periodically sweep the room while you give the audience a "hug" with your eyes.

This is not as easy as it appears. Be aware of these pitfalls:

- ✓ Avoid gazing above or below audience eye level. Look right at them.
- ✓ Avoid eye-surfing (darting back and forth for short periods of time, never gluing into any one person for the steady three to five seconds).
- ✓ Avoid directing your eyes toward your notes, flip chart, or transparency for too long. The audience wants your attention. Talk to the audience, not to your visual aids. Notes are fine, but scoop up your thoughts quickly, then return your attention to the audience.

Great eye contact is one of those special skills that is a *really big deal*. People who use eyeball-to-eyeball connection are perceived as trustworthy, confident, friendly, and caring. It's a valuable skill to perfect, not only in presentations, but in everyday life!

56. Take Up Space

The more space you take up, the more powerful you look. Think of being in the center seat on an airplane. Who dominates the armrest? Look at a man sitting and a woman sitting. Who takes up more space?

When making presentations, take firm and energetic command over the space in the room. Don't lock yourself in a single position. Move it! Move around the room. Move at least two steps at a time. If you move only one step at a time, it will look as though you're rocking or doing the cha-cha. Give yourself some reasons to move. Go over to a flip chart or overhead projector. When I speak, I like to have a small table on my right side for notes (that's my "note station"). Then I use a flip chart (my "flip chart station"). Finally, I have an area close to the audience where I make important points, answer questions, engage in discussions. This is the "just-you-and-me station." It's a special place that lets me connect heart-to-heart with the people in the audience. By having specific places to go in the room, I can walk around with both energy and purpose.

Your hands and arms need to take up space. Get your armpits out, elbows away from your side, and gesture like you really mean it (not limp and floppy). One of my clients' most frequent concerns is, "What should I do with my arms?" People usually have no clue as to what to do with those appendages. Tall people, especially, are very reluctant to gesture. Their long arms make them feel as though their wings will be flapping if they use large gestures.

My solution for gesture paralysis is to use "hallway gestures." Imagine that you are standing out in the hallway talking to your buddy about last night's game. You're probably using natural, expressive, uninhibited gestures that convey your true feelings. In presentations, too, feel the message. Let the message penetrate into your fingers and toes. The gestures will follow.

57. Don't Get Stuck

Here's a hit list of frozen positions that will detract from your message and your look of confidence. Avoid them.

+ The fig leaf (hands covering genitals)
+ Hail Mary (hands in prayer position)
+ Drill sergeant (arms folded in front)
+ Parade rest (hands clenched in back)
+ Hands in pockets
+ The leaner
+ The hip hugger (hands on hips)
+ Podium police (hands clutching podium)

Note: If you find yourself in one of the above positions, it's best to let your arms hang loosely by your side. This is the most powerful-looking neutral position. Also, if you don't let your hands touch, you'll usually stay out of trouble.

If you choose to use a lectern or podium, can you still look dynamic? The answer is yes, if you pretend that it isn't there. Continue to gesture above the podium and to the side. Don't clutch the podium. However, the only benefit of the podium is as a place to hold your notes (especially for tall people). Don't think that you can hide behind it. Pivot your body from time to time to look at various parts of the room. Your eye contact needs to be especially strong to overcome the physical barrier of the podium. Removal of the podium will increase the perception of friendliness. I don't like podiums. They create a wall between a speaker and the audience. My preference: Get rid of the podium.

58. Avoid Fiddling, Fidgeting, and Flagrant Fouls

Most speakers are guilty of some distracting mannerisms from time to time. Be aware of your potential pitfalls and correct them on the spot. Keep the audience focused on you and your message, not on distractions. Audiences report that these distracters are so annoying that they can detract from your presentation (sometimes to the point that their interest is completely lost).

Each time I see myself on video, there is usually some type of mannerism that I need to wipe out of my repertoire. Once I was bobbing my head like a little football player doll on the back ledge of someone's car. Another time I was rising up on my toes like a ballerina each time I made a point. Once I became aware of the offense, I could put a halt to it.

Here are some distracters that have been identified in my audience research:

+ Coins jingling in pockets
+ Snorting
+ Playing with tie or jewelry
+ Fiddling with hair, beard, or mustache
+ Chewing ice
+ Toying with glasses

- Tapping a pen or pencil
- Snapping a marker cap on and off
- Rolling eyes up to the ceiling
- Excessive blinking
- Playing with a pointer

59. Show Your Glow (Smile!)

Often I'm asked this question: "I'm not saying anything funny, so should I still smile?" The answer is simple: *yes!* Smiling when you're tense and concentrating on your message is not easy. However, it's one of the most important things you can do. It's a *big deal* to the audience. Smiling lets the audience know that you're friendly, that you like them, and that you care about the topic. *That's big stuff!*

Johnny Miller, the famous golfer, had difficulty relating to the gallery. In fact, many of his fans deserted him. Johnny admitted that he had a hard time concentrating on his game and paying attention to the crowd at the same time. He was advised to wave and smile as he walked down the fairway and after he holed every putt. Instantly, the crowd warmed up to him. They responded and applauded, and his galleries grew. By the way, it didn't hurt his game, either.

Beyond smiling, animate your face. Use your eyebrows, eyes, cheeks, mouth, lips, nose, neck, and teeth to express emotion. Often, before a presentation, your face will feel very tense. If that's the case, find a place where you can hide, and do some "face aerobics." I call this Comedy and Tragedy (after the famed theatrical symbols). First, stretch out your face as far as it will go and laugh heartily (comedy). Then scrunch your face and pretend that you are weeping (tragedy). Alternate between the two for about thirty seconds: comedy . . . tragedy . . . comedy . . . tragedy . . . You will be surprised at the release of facial tension. When I first start this exercise, my face feels as though it is going to crack, the muscles are so tight and tense.

A few years ago I worked with an executive who wanted to change his stiff and stuffy image. He wanted people to see him as a friendly person. Smiling was something that he had to consciously think about, so he pasted "happy face" stickers throughout his presentation notes.

60. Stretch Your Style

My natural presentation style is very lively and outgoing. I walk around a lot, use a loud voice, and gesture almost constantly. If I spoke with that intensity all day, I would surely exhaust the audience (and myself, too). Therefore, I like to add variety to my style by calming down, speaking more slowly, using just a few gestures. Maybe I'll even sit down for part of the presentation to lower the intensity. This gives both the audience and me a very welcome rest. It also heightens their attention, because I am un-predictable.

Another way to expand your style is to use a variety of au-diovisual aids. Use props, the flip chart, an overhead projector, charts, handouts, videos. Each time you change the method of visual presentation, the audience becomes more attentive. There's nothing worse than a presenter using an overhead pro-jector for two hours straight!

After I work with people in my two-day Speakers Training Camp, they always want to know how they can continue to im-prove. My advice is to pick one or two things that will make the most significant difference in your presentation style. Then monitor yourself on how you're doing. You can write cue words in the margins of your notes as reminders. You might have the words LOUDER! or EYES! or SMILE! or ENERGY! or MOVE ARMS! An-other great way to change your behavior is to put your watch on the opposite wrist. It will act as a great memory trigger. Remem-ber that it may take months to completely incorporate one of these skills into your natural repertoire.

Even if you present frequently, always take an honest look at yourself. Maybe you're a trademark storyteller. That's great, but start pushing yourself. Add more humor, props, or other devices. Target a few areas in which you can expand your style. Monitor yourself (sometimes with audio and video recordings). After each presentation, rate your target area on a scale of one to ten.

61. Evaluate Your Style

You can become your own best coach. Give your style a frequent checkup. The best way is to tape a presentation or practice session with a video recorder and then analyze the results. If you don't have someone to operate the camera, that's OK. You can set the camera up on a tripod in the back of the room and then just let it roll. During your review of the tape, use the following checklist as a guide.

   - ✓ *Gestures:* Lively and comfortable, avoided getting stuck in one position
   - ✓ Smile (lots of it)
   - ✓ Eye contact: Three- to five-second mini-conversations
   - ✓ Voice: Lively and energetic
   - ✓ Pause: Used lots of pauses effectively
   - ✓ Volume: Appropriate for the size of the group
   - ✓ Volume: Varied loud and soft
   - ✓ Appeared confident
   - ✓ Avoided distracting mannerisms
   - ✓ Whole body movement: Used the space well; did not pace
   - ✓ Facial expression: The face was a messenger for the message, not stone-faced
   - ✓ Appearance: Stood out among the crowd; appropriately dressed, used good color, quality; accessory drew attention to the face (tie, bold jewelry)

Chapter 7

Master the Magic in Your Voice

Have you ever developed a strong impression of someone you've communicated with only over the phone? Have you ever been shocked when you finally met that person? Vocal impressions account for a large portion of overall image. Few people think about using the voice to its full capacity. You can have the best sales presentation, the best multimedia gadgetry, and the finest Italian suit, but if your voice sounds dull and boring, you will be perceived as dull and boring. Audiences rank enthusiasm as one of their top three requirements for a great speaker. Enthusiasm is judged partly through the voice. The worst thing a presenter can do (in the minds of the audience) is to have a monotone voice. In this chapter, you'll learn how to expand your vocal skills to convey a more enthusiastic, convincing, and memorable message.

What makes Alfred Hitchcock's voice sound different from Howard Cosell's? A great deal is dependent on the physical "cards" you've been dealt: the size and shape of your mouth, throat, nose, and the mass around the vocal cords. But, you can make changes!

Often, people are surprised at how easy it is to add more enthusiasm, create more interest, or sound more confident by just making a few vocal adjustments. Imagine that your voice is like a radio. By tuning the various controls, such as speed, volume, and pitch, you can change the perception of your voice. It's easy. All you have to do is:

62. Breathe Low and Slow
63. Check the Speed Limit
64. Trash Your Vocal Garbage
65. Pitch It Low and Wide
66. Gauge Your Gusto
67. Pause to Punctuate a Point
68. Speak From Your Heart
69. Change the Beat
70. Develop Your Vocal Uniqueness
71. Take Good Care of Your Voice

"My favorite presenter was an ex-ballplayer. He had such a commanding voice. Within the first few words you wanted to stay focused on what he was going to say."

—General Manager

62. Breathe Low and Slow

Breathing is your energy source for speaking. It is the foundation for relaxation and helps to control volume. Knowing how to breathe correctly is at the core of vocal control and strength.

There are two ways to breathe. Take a deep breath. If your shoulders go up and down, you are doing what is called chest breathing or shallow breathing. This is the wrong way to do it. Now breathe deeply and make your stomach go in and out. Put your hand on your stomach and feel it going in and out. In fact, if you're really relaxed, you'll be able to feel your back and entire midsection go in and out. This is called diaphragm breathing or deep breathing. The diaphragm is located below the lower rib cage. Diaphragm breathing provides a much more efficient and effective flow of air.

Approximately 25 percent of the people I work with have problems with proper breathing during their presentations. The difficulties caused by incorrect breathing are many: breathlessness (which gives the impression of nervousness), hoarseness, and vocal tension. The alternative, a relaxed energy source, is simple: *breathe low and slow*. Take a full, deep breath generated from the diaphragm area (low), and breathe slowly.

One of the questions I'm frequently asked is this: "What do I do if I'm in front of a group, and I suddenly realize I'm out of breath?" This is a common problem. There are a few things you can do to ease the tension. First, pause. Be sure to inhale and exhale completely during that pause. Slow down your rate of speaking for a while. Finally, to regain your composure, turn the attention over to the audience. Get them involved. It will take all of the pressure off you. For example, if it's a small group, you can ask the audience members to each respond to a question related to the topic: "Let's go around the room, and I'd like to find out what problems you're currently having with the new computer training program." If it's a large group, you can have the individuals discuss the same issue with two other people nearby.

If you typically get out of breath during the opening of your talk, plan on starting with some type of audience involvement. After several minutes of audience interaction, you'll be able to continue your presentation with ease.

63. Check the Speed Limit

What speed is just right? It depends—in what part of the country are you speaking? Always think about the natural speed limit. Speed up in New York and Chicago. Slow down in Atlanta and Dallas. Pay attention to your surroundings. Audiences like speakers whose style blends with their own, and that includes how fast you speak. Perceptions can sometimes be cruel. A fast-paced New Yorker with a Brooklyn accent speaking in Oregon might be perceived as sharp, cold, and digital. A speaker from Dallas with a southern twang speaking in New York might be perceived as casual and countrified. If you want to increase your chances of audience compatibility, adapt to the pace of your environment.

During the 1992 presidential debates, my ten-year-old daughter looked at the TV, pointed to Ross Perot, and asked, "Who's that, Mom?" I said, "That's Ross Perot; he's running for president." She then said, "Gee—he sounds like a guy who should be selling barbecue sauce." I was amazed that vocal impressions had such an effect on a ten-year-old.

Be aware of your natural rate of speaking. Is it slow, fast, or just right? If necessary, adjust your speed to match the needs of your audience. If you are presenting complicated material, or if you speak with a foreign accent, speak a little slower. If you are showing emotion, speak faster. The secret to creating an interesting pace is to vary it. Don't speak at the same rate all the time. Be unpredictable! Zig Zigler, the famous motivational speaker, is a champion at slowing down and drawing out his words for extra emphasis.

Just as speaking too fast can create a problem, speaking too slowly can also be a hazard. An extremely slow rate of speech makes the speaker seem uninterested in the material. The audience members then will think, "If the speaker isn't interested in this, why should *I* be interested in it?" Also, their minds will wander, and it will be harder for them to pay attention, especially if slow speech is combined with a monotone voice.

The key factors to remember are:

1. Be aware of your natural speed.
2. Vary the speed depending on audience needs.
3. Change the speed frequently to create interest in your presentation.

It's like taking a trip with your voice. Sometimes the speed limit is 55 MPH, and other times it's 35 MPH. And don't forget to stop at the red lights!

64. Trash Your Vocal Garbage

Audiences include "vocal garbage" among the top ten sins committed by presenters. There are several different types of vocal garbage. There are nonwords, such as "um," "uh," and "and-uh." There are overused words, the same word repeated over and over again in a talk. A presenter might get on an "OK" kick or repeat the word "excellent" ten times in a half-hour. Other speakers might insert lip smacking, throat clearing, sniffing, or snorting between thoughts. All of these types of vocal garbage are distractions to the audience.

Almost all presenters have a pet offense, and they are completely unaware of what they are doing. How do you fix the problem?

1. Become aware of any type of vocal garbage that you are using.
2. Replace the garbage with a pause. Remember that audiences like pauses and do not like vocal garbage. Subconsciously, presenters think that if they are to appear organized and intelligent, there has to be constant verbalization during a presentation. That's not true. It's OK to pause. You don't need to fill up every little inch of air space with sound. So, if you need to think momentarily, or if you lose your place, just pause *silently*! A pause is the only replacement for vocal garbage.
3. If you know that you have a problem with saying "uh," for example, you can write or draw reminders to yourself in the margin of your notes:
4. Use simple, easy notes and audiovisuals. It will help you to stay organized and focused.
5. Continually monitor your progress with the use of a video camera or tape recorder, or ask your friends for some feedback.

65. Pitch It Low and Wide

Imagine the sound of Mickey Mouse's voice. Now imagine that voice delivering the evening news. How believable and enjoyable would it be? Instead, imagine the voice of your favorite nightly newscaster. He or she probably has a much lower voice than Mickey Mouse. The difference is what we call *pitch*—how high or low the voice is.

In the world of business, a low voice is pure gold. People with lower voices are perceived as more intelligent, more authoritative, and more powerful than those with higher voices. People with higher voices are considered to be weaker, less reliable, and less confident. Women normally have higher voices than men, but even within the realm of female voices, those of female TV and radio broadcasters are usually in the lower range.

If you think your voice is too high, you can lower it by working with a tape recorder or contact a speech pathologist for a vocal analysis.

Lowering your pitch at the end of a sentence adds authority to what you're saying. Raising your voice at the end of a sentence means that you are asking a question or seeking approval. Avoid curling your voice up at the end of the sentence when you are not asking a question—for example: "We have three people on the strategy team? And they just went through training? Now they're ready to start training the others?" In this case, a question is not being asked. Therefore, the voice should be lowered, not raised, at the end of the sentence. Otherwise, all authority in the sentence is lost.

Imagine that the sounds in your voice are plotted on a musical scale. The most interesting voices use a wide range of notes, both high and low. If your voice has a narrow range, you will sound monotone. Let the energy of your message dictate the pulse of your voice.

66. Gauge Your Gusto

I once worked with a training manager whose voice was barely audible to ten people in a small room. When the audience, a group of strangers, was asked for their initial impressions of this manager, the group said that she seemed to be shy, unsure of herself, and nervous. In reality, the manager was a top-notch, well-respected individual. But because of her extremely soft voice, she was not perceived positively while delivering presentations.

I faced a real challenge in helping this person increase the volume of her voice. We went into a huge hotel ballroom. With the help of a tape recorder, we started to work. I used a recorder with lights that flash during vocalization. In order to keep the lights flashing, you need a certain amount of volume. When the volume is weak, the lights stop flashing. This is a great visual way to see how loud a speaker's voice is. First, I had the training manager say the sound "ah" close to the recorder. Then, saying the same sound, she kept moving back further and further from the recorder until she could successfully make the lights flash from a distance of twenty-five yards. We then repeated this same activity with increasing lengths of utterance. From a single sound, she progressed to single words, then phrases, then sentences, then conversation.

Typically, when people are working on increasing the volume of their voice, they feel like they are shouting. It is usually very difficult for them to push the sound out. Usually their source of energy is from the throat area. Instead, they need to be retrained to bring the sound up from the diaphragm (lower rib cage).

An average speaker can speak loud enough to be heard, without a microphone, in a room holding about sixty people. Carefully adjust the volume of your voice to suit the size of the group. Then, add some dramatics and vary it. Crank up the volume to convey excitement. Reduce the sound to a whisper when you want to express heartfelt conviction.

67. Pause to Punctuate a Point

One of the most effective things a speaker can say is:

 NOTHING

Use a pause to emphasize a point, make a transition from one thought to another, and promote audience interaction. This sounds easy, but it's not! It's very difficult for presenters to give up the spotlight for the sake of silence. However, a pause has an engaging effect on the audience and is well worth the effort. Often, if they do pause, speakers make the mistake of not pausing long enough.

Here are some examples of effective pauses:

"He had only one problem. . . . He couldn't tell the truth."
"What do you think his answer was? . . . His father always
   lied to the kids."

Here are some key points to remember in creating effective pauses. Speakers usually don't pause long enough for maximum effect. Approximately three to four seconds (inhale and exhale) is an adequate pause time. Be sure to add steady eye contact during the pause. If you are facilitating a group, leading a meeting, or posing questions and answers to the audience, the need for pause increases. In these cases, a twenty-second pause is sometimes needed. When you ask a question, actually count to twenty in your head. For the presenter, it feels like an eternity. But for the members of the audience, it is merely a signal to think and respond.

68. Speak From Your Heart

When I ask audiences what they like best about speakers, the word *passion* is often mentioned. Listen to Tom Peters, the famous *In Search of Excellence* guru. He shouts. His voice cracks with excitement. He cares. He speaks from his heart. He allows his deep convictions about the topic to explode through his voice. There's no holding back. He also uses body language that matches his fervor—pacing, sweating, tousled hair.

Whether you're speaking about fighting crime or selling running shoes, let your feelings for the subject be heard through an energized voice—one that matches the message. Change the volume (loud and soft); change the pitch (high and low); change the rate (fast and slow). Vocal variety is the secret. Most of all, let your feelings be heard. The audience will pick up on your passion (or lack of it) and attach it to the subject of your talk.

There are two ways to increase the passion:

1. Work on the voice itself. Practice with a tape recorder. Read some poetry or a children's book, and venture to the extremes with your voice. Ham it up! Stretch it out! See how far you can go with your vocal range. Then gradually start putting more conviction into your presentations. If you're really serious about expanding your vocal capabilities, take an acting class.

2. Replace the dull sections of your presentation with something that gets you fired up: a funny story, an example of a re-

cent success, a letter from a delighted customer, a gripping account of a kidnapping case, an interesting demonstration of your products. When you jazz up the material, you will naturally jazz up your voice and your entire style.

69. Change the Beat

Variety, variety, variety. You've been reading that word throughout this entire chapter. In describing vocal energy, it's the single most important word. The audience will tire of a speaker who is stuck on the same beat for too long. A laid-back, mellow speaker needs to crank up the energy from time to time to keep the audience interested. In contrast, a high-energy presenter needs to calm down, back off, and slow down occasionally. Varying the beat creates great contrast within the message, and the audience will cling to every word.

Let's take a closer look at exactly how a speaker does this. John Bradshaw, a popular speaker on "Healing the Inner Child," uses lots of vocal variety in his style, which is primarily high-energy. Here's an analysis of his voice:

Passionate:	He makes changes in volume (loud and soft). His voice sometimes cracks during emotional moments. He makes changes in pitch (high and low). There is no doubt that he really cares about his subject.
Convincing:	He punctuates his words with extra emphasis. Again, he uses volume and pitch changes.
Knowledgeable:	He uses an extensive vocabulary, with clear and correct pronunciation of words. There is very little vocal garbage. The volume is quite loud and forceful.
Motivating:	He makes changes in pitch and volume while relating stories from his own childhood, uses pauses for emphasis,

and slows down when making major points.

70. Develop Your Vocal Uniqueness

Angela Lansbury is identified by a British accent. Arnold Palmer has a soft, country style. Jesse Jackson has a loud, fervent, resonant voice. These three personalities have distinctive styles that are different, recognizable, and very likable. What makes your voice unique? Here are some ideas to help you develop your own vocal identity:

1. Find out what makes your voice different from those of the five people sitting next to you. Record their voices and identify the distinctive characteristics.

2. Pay attention to the way people perceive your voice. When you get phone calls at work, if the caller asks to speak to the boss (and you *are* the boss), you're in trouble! What is your telephone image? After only hearing your voice on the phone, do people think you are older? taller? smarter? more successful? richer? tired? excitable? Are you pleased with those first phone impressions? I have a naturally loud, strong, no-nonsense type of voice. When people meet me in person, they often say that they expected me to be taller. I am pleased with that vocal image, because the perception is that a loud voice is associated with height, which is associated with strength and authority. I also realize that it is necessary for me at times to back off from that very strong and forceful image. I need to soften my voice, turn down the volume, and calm down.

3. Assess your own vocal strengths and weaknesses; then, make the necessary changes. If your voice is:

- *Monotone and boring:* Increase your vocal energy with volume changes, pitch changes, and rate changes.
- *Nasal:* Open your mouth and talk from the back of your throat.
- *Childlike:* Lower your pitch; check your vocabulary.
- *Stiff and stuffy:* Use more vocal energy, create a greater

range of sound, from excited to soft and caring (smile
with your voice).

+ *Intimidating:* Lower the volume, slow down, pause, soften
   the sound.

Listen to your own voice on a cassette recorder or on your answering machine or voice mail. What do you like? What changes
would you like to make?

71. Take Good Care of Your Voice

No voice . . . no message. Here are some tips on keeping your
voice in top condition:

- ✓ Don't abuse your voice by shouting. It can cause recurring
  hoarseness, which can lead to vocal nodules (bumps on
  the vocal cords). Screaming for your favorite NBA team
  the night before a presentation is not a good idea.
- ✓ Don't smoke. Besides the risk of cancer, smoking causes
  an undesirable raspy sound in the voice. It can also cause
  shortness of breath and coughing.
- ✓ Do drink lots of water, hot liquids, and lemon while you
  are speaking. It keeps your voice lubricated. Avoid ice;
  it will tighten your vocal cords. Lemon juice works well,
  especially if you have a cold.
- ✓ Avoid milk products. They produce phlegm in the throat.
- ✓ If you have a soft voice, use a microphone whenever you
  can. If you do a lot of speaking, you can purchase a com-
  pact wireless mike that is very convenient. A mike will
  enhance the "star" quality in your voice.
- ✓ Get plenty of rest. When you are tired, your voice will
  sound tired and hoarse.
- ✓ If you have a noticeable problem with your voice—too
  high, too soft, nasal and whiny, hoarse—seek the professional help of a speech pathologist.
- ✓ Get your voice in shape by doing vocal exercises before
  your presentation.

Chapter 8
Create Exciting
Visual Aids

David Peoples, in his book *Presentations Plus*, says that people gain 75 percent of what they know visually, 13 percent through hearing, and 12 percent through smell, touch, and taste. Research shows that about 85 percent of the information stored in the brain is received visually. Information that is *seen* has a much greater chance of being remembered than information that is *heard*. Since many people are visually oriented, it is critical that presentations include visual aids such as flip charts, overhead transparencies, slide shows, computer-generated graphics, props, or handouts.

Visual aids, however, are never a replacement for the presenter. *You* are still the number 1 visual in your presentation. Your connection to the audience, your energy, your charisma are more important than any piece of multimedia equipment! Always keep that in perspective. In fact, only two people from the Memorable Speaker Survey mentioned visual aids when describing their favorite presenter.

Visual aids benefit the audience. They can:

+ Aid in retention
+ Clarify a point
+ Focus attention
+ Create interest

Visual aids also benefit the presenter. They can:

+ Increase the look of professionalism
+ Help to organize thoughts

+ Be used as notes
+ Give the presenter a reason to move around

In this chapter, you'll learn to:

72. Create Simple Visuals
73. Avoid the Tiny-Cluttered-Numbers Syndrome
74. Keep Your Visuals Visible
75. Add Spontaneous Flair With Flip Charts
76. Supercharge Your Overhead Transparencies
77. Control Your Overhead Show
78. Electrify Your Presentation: Videos, Slides, Computer-Generated Shows
79. Reinforce Details With Handy Handouts
80. Test! Test! And Test Again!
81. Glow, Even When the Lights Go Out

"Don't even think about using tables and charts that are too complicated or too small to read."

—Field Department Manager

72. Create Simple Visuals

If it looks good on a T-shirt, it will look good as a visual aid. In other words, keep it simple! There are four basic rules to remember: Use big, bold letters, keep the design simple, use two or three colors, and add pictures and graphs when possible.

Be sure that your graphic is clear, interesting, simple, and visible. Figure 8-1 illustrates these rules and their application.

73. Avoid the Tiny-Cluttered-Numbers Syndrome

If someone asked me to identify the number-1 problem with visual aids, it would definitely be the tiny-cluttered-numbers syndrome. The numbers are usually typed, then photocopied

Figure 8-1. Good, better, best rules for visuals.

Good

Rules for Visuals
Great visuals have big, simple, colorful pictures.

Better

Rules for Visuals
• Big • Simple • Colorful • Pictures

Best

Rules for Visuals
• Big • Simple • Colorful • Pictures

onto a transparency. You've seen transparencies like this before. They look like the one shown in Figure 8-2.

Audiences dislike the confusion of cluttered visuals. They can't read the details. Instead, the visual should contain a clear, basic idea, like that in Figure 8-3.

"A picture is worth a thousand words, but a picture of a thousand words ain't worth much"—Unknown (but very wise).

74. Keep Your Visuals Visible

Sounds simple, doesn't it? Yet 50 percent of all visual aids cannot be seen for the reasons shown in Figure 8-4.

Figure 8-2. Transparency suffering from tiny-cluttered-numbers syndrome.

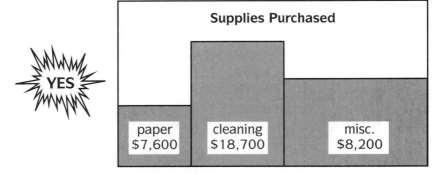

Supplies Purchased			
Supplier	Item	Cost–$	Projection
DQX	Note Cards	3,000	0
Fred Link	Stationery	4,600	2,200
Johnson	Wax	15,500	16,000
Dove	Soap	3,200	4,000
Daltons	Books	3,900	9,500
Wise	Tires	4,300	7,000

Figure 8-3. Clear, uncluttered transparency.

Supplies Purchased

paper $7,600   cleaning $18,700   misc. $8,200

75. Add Spontaneous Flair With Flip Charts

Visual Aid: Flip chart

Size of Audience: 1 to 40

Preparation: Whether or not you prepare the flip charts before your presentation is a matter of personal choice. Some presenters prefer having everything written and drawn ahead of time; others prefer to write spontaneously as they speak. Audiences show no preference. If you have trouble staying on track and organizing your presentation, it will be to your advantage to prepare the charts ahead of time.

Figure 8-4. Common reasons that visual aids cannot be seen.

Tiny Type

What if this type was so small that no one could possibly read it.
That would be a waste of time and energy. Not to mention a real problem. What if this type was so small that no one could possibly read it.
That would be a waste of time and energy. Not to mention a real problem what if this type was so small that no one could possibly read it. Wait a minute, we can't read this copy. That would be a waste of time and energy. Not to nmention a real problem. The type is much too small to read. What if this type was so small that no one could possible read it. That would be a waste of time and energy. Not to mention a real problem. What if this type was so small that no one could possibly read it.
That would be a waste of time and energy. Not to mention a real problem. what if this type was so small that no one could possibly read it. Wait a minute, we can't read this copy. That would be a waste of time and energy.

Blocking the View

Insider's Tips:

1. Practice turning the pages. It takes some coordination.
2. Paper with lines will help you to write straighter.
3. Use "Mr. Sketch" water-based markers.
4. Black, blue, purple, and red have the best visibility.
5. Pencil in notes on the chart to jog your memory.
6. Do not write on the bottom 20 percent of the chart—it's hard to see.
7. Staple two pieces of flip-chart paper together at the bottom of the page to eliminate the see-through effect.
8. Use no more than six lines on a page.
9. Flip charts are great for use in brainstorming activities, writing key words, or drawing simple diagrams. You do not need to be a great artist in order to get your point across.
10. For larger audiences, you can put the flip chart on a platform or riser for greater visibility.

Sue's Opinion: I love flip charts. They are tops in user friendliness. I use them whenever possible. Even if you use other types of A-V equipment, put a flip chart in the room and use it occasionally. It will add personalized flair and interest to your talk.

76. Supercharge Your Overhead Transparencies

Visual Aid: Overhead projector and transparencies

Size of Audience: 1 to 200

Preparation: With fancy computer graphics packages, your transparencies can look dazzling. With materials that can be photocopied or run through a computer printer, they are quick and easy to develop. Prepare all of your work horizontally. To ensure that your transparencies are straight when you place them on the projector, use masking tape as a guide right on the projector, 3-M flip frames (sleeves that encase the transparency), cardboard mounts, or "Insta-Frame," a rectangular device that is seated on the projector. Number each transparency—just in case you drop them on the floor!

Insider's Tips:

1. Turn the projector off when not in use. You can also use a piece of cardboard to cover the light. Some projectors come with a device that shields the light. Another idea is to put a dark piece of paper on the projector instead of a transparency until you are ready to begin again.
2. Cheat! You can write notes around the transparency frames.
3. Use *big, simple lettering and pictures.* (Typed letters will not show up.)
4. Use blank transparencies and special wipe-off pens for a spontaneous effect. These pens can also add some spontaneity to prewritten transparencies.
6. Use a pencil, pen, or swizzle stick to point directly to the transparency to explain an idea. If you point to the screen, usually your back will be facing the audience.
7. Teachers' supply stores are great places for inspiration for inexpensive graphics.
8. Be sure to arrive early. Test the machine. Focus it. Have your first transparency on the screen and ready to go.

Sue's Opinion: An overhead projector competes with you. The bright light and the sound of some machines can grab the audience's attention. It is not an audience-friendly piece of equipment. In fact, when the machine is turned off, a feeling of relaxation usually occurs. I suggest that you use the overhead projector for a maximum of twenty minutes at a time. Turn the machine off and do something else for about ten minutes before you use the overhead projector again.

77. Control Your Overhead Show

Have the first transparency on the projector, focused and ready to go, before you start your presentation. See Figure 8-5.

Figure 8-5. Make sure the first transparency is ready to go and *focused*.

The best setup for your projector is a six-foot table and screen positioned across the corner of the room (diagonally), as shown in Figure 8-6. If you are right-handed, the table should be on your right as you face the audience. This will give you plenty of room for your materials. A little projector cart isn't big enough.

Use a triangular flow to move transparencies onto and off the projector. Use a three-point arrangement (see Figure 8-7): Point 1 is the unused transparencies in a pile, point 2 is the overhead projector with the transparency in use, and point 3 is the used transparencies in a pile. Move your transparencies in the same direction all the time, to successive points of the triangle.

78. Electrify Your Presentation: Videos, Slides, Computer-Generated Shows

Visual Aids: Slides, videos, computer-generated shows, films

Figure 8-6. Best setup for projector and screen.

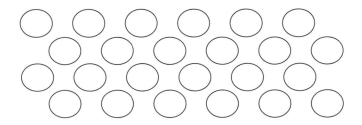

Six-foot table with projector

Preparation: Lots! The computer world blesses us with new options daily. As technological features are added, preparation time increases. Razzle-dazzle can create frazzle-frazzle if the presenter is not well prepared and completely familiar with the equipment. Hiring an audiovisuals expert for the design and production of these visuals and for the operation of equipment during the presentation is always an option. Either really know your stuff or hire someone who does.

Insider's Tips:

1. Remember that you, not the technology, are the number-1 connection to the audience.
2. Always start and end the presentation with full lighting.

Figure 8-7. Three-point arrangement for moving transparencies onto and off the projector.

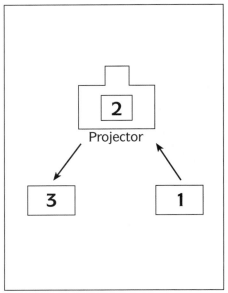

3. For the first and last three minutes, it should be just you and the audience—no electronic media.
4. If the room must be dark, use a lectern light or spotlight shining on your face.
5. Stick with your style. Even though the audience's attention is often focused on the visual, you still need to smile, move, and sound enthusiastic.
6. Let the visuals flow smoothly and swiftly. Don't get caught up in whistles, bells, dissolves, and on-screen explosions.

Sue's Opinion: I have seen many computer-generated presentation shows, but I have seen only two that were done efficiently and effectively. Most often, the presenters hit snags in the cueing of visuals and spend too much time with the fancy graphics instead of the message. Many of these presentations appear cumbersome, and lack any sense of rhythm. Always remember that you are the show. Visual aids should complement you, not the other way around.

79. Reinforce Details With Handy Handouts

Visual Aid: Handouts (including workbooks, manuals, flyers, pamphlets, ball caps, pens, pins, and laminated pocket cards).

Preparation: Handouts allow great opportunities for variety and creativity. Be sure that your handouts mirror your own image. For example, you wouldn't use a ten-page stapled booklet for a $1,000 seminar. Length, cost, and detail are really your choice.

Insider's Tips:

1. Every presentation should have some type of handout to reinforce the message. Have some fun. Think beyond written pages, stapled at the left!
2. Keep written handouts simple. What do you want the audience to remember one month down the road?
3. Put "extras" in the handout that you don't have time to cover during the presentation: bibliography, extra details, extra examples, sources for more information.
4. Fill-in-the-blank pages can be used for audience interaction.
5. If the audience has no need to refer to the written handout during your presentation, tell them that they will be getting it at the end of the session. That way you won't be competing with the handout for the audience's attention.
6. Use your handout as a marketing tool. Put your name and address on it.
7. Themes and key phrases can be put on key chains, pens, ball caps, and other such items. They help your audience remember the message.

Sue's Opinion: A handout is a must for every session. The audience needs something to take with them. The best handouts are simple, short, and usable. My favorites are: a one-page summary of main points, a three-ring binder with the title on the spine, a pen holder for my desk, a magnetic refrigerator calendar, a ball cap.

80. Test! Test! And Test Again!

Become a fanatical tester. Test all of your audiovisual equipment prior to your presentation (even if it's the same overhead projector you've used for the past fifteen years). Arrive early and try everything: turn it on, adjust it, focus it, and give it a trial run. Be aware of these potential pitfalls:

- ✓ *Flip chart:* Check for stability (some are very wobbly); test the markers for dryness.
- ✓ *Overhead projector:* Check focus and visibility by the entire audience (stand in the back of the room and take a look at what they will be seeing). Turn the projector on and off. Be sure there is a spare bulb, and know how to change it.
- ✓ *Slide projector:* Test-drive at least ten slides. Check the focus and visibility.
- ✓ *VCR:* Play a few minutes of videotape; know where the controls are, become familiar with the buttons on the remote, adjust the volume, stop, rewind, pause. Check the tracking; cue the tape for the precise starting point. Some machines create a loud, annoying hiss until the tape has run for a few seconds. If this is the case, keep the volume down at first and increase it after the tape has played for a short time. When you are finished, turn off the TV first, then the VCR.
- ✓ *Computer graphics:* Check the visibility. Run through about three minutes worth of graphics and any special effects and features you'll be using.
- ✓ *Microphone:* All mikes are different. Some need to be spoken into directly; others will pick up sound from all directions. Request the type of mike you prefer: lavaliere, hand-held, wireless, or attached to the lectern. Speak into the mike and do a sound check with someone standing in the back of the room.
- ✓ *Room setup:* Be sure that your directions for the setup of the room are clear and in writing. Give your contact person a drawing of exactly what you want. Always arrive early enough to change the setup if needed.
- ✓ *Writing devices:* Bring your own markers and transpar-

ency pens—90 percent of the time, the ones provided are dry.

✓ *Light switches:* Find out where they are, and know how to use them.

Sue's Opinion: Never become overconfident when it comes time for an equipment check. In the audience's eyes, you are responsible (even if the A-V department set up the equipment). Always arrive early and test everything.

81. Glow, Even When the Lights Go Out

What will you do when the equipment fails?

One day the lights went out on popular socio-psychologist Jennifer James. She was speaking to about 500 dentists when the entire room went dark, except for small emergency bulbs around the room. There was no electricity in the entire hotel. The overhead projector and microphone were no longer functional. Jennifer couldn't even see a page of notes! What did she do? She walked into the center of the room, cranked up her voice projection, adopted a theater-in-the-round delivery, and proceeded. She knew her material and her organization well enough to ad lib through the main points. She was very conversational and made the best of an awkward situation. The audience was truly impressed.

Here are some tips for "presentation insurance":

✓ *Always have a back-up plan.* You need to proceed regardless of any equipment malfunction. Apologize once and move on. Know your material. Add some audience involvement. Think of carrying on a conversation with the audience.

✓ *When traveling by air, keep your visuals and notes with you.* Do not check them with your luggage.

Sue's Opinion: Equipment problems will happen. The audience will forgive you. They will understand. What's most important is how you deal with the problem. Are you calm and professional, or are you shriveling with fear and embarrassment? If you are prepared for possible problems, there should be no difference in the end result of your presentation. All you need to know is: *What will you do when the equipment fails?*

Chapter 9

Bulletproof Your Presentation

Your presentation is floating along flawlessly (you think). You're on cruise control. Then reality deals you a frightening blow. As you look out into the audience, you are stunned. Five people are sitting with their heads propped on their hands, fifteen in the front row seem to be unconscious, there's a group chatting in the right corner, and seven others yawn simultaneously. In the words of Dennis the Menace, "Yipes!"

Congratulations. At least you recognized that there's a problem. Some speakers are so self-absorbed that they are oblivious to audiences' signs of boredom. Now that you know that there's a problem, you're ready to bail out of the negative situation, and turn it around so the audience is reenergized, reactivated, and really interested. If you can do that, you are a champion presenter! In this chapter, you'll learn *presentation C.P.R.:*

1. Check the pulse.
2. Pinpoint the problem.
3. Recover.

I began writing this chapter while flying to Phoenix for my two-day Speakers Training Camp, and I certainly used my own advice. My carefully chosen workshop site turned out to be the "hotel from hell." In twelve years of training, I had never experienced a disaster of this magnitude. The executive from Hewlett-Packard had no bed in his room—just a couch; the accountant from Seattle had no running water; the staff had no idea what U-shape seating was, and the busboys barged into the meeting five times during the morning session. By using C.P.R., I saved the day (and my reputation). I checked the pulse of the group (slowly dying). I pinpointed the problem (bad hotel choice). I recovered (opened the program with comments about "the hotel from hell," apologized, located the swankiest hotel during the lunch hour, and changed the workshop site). The end result: glowing evaluations and repeat business. (Whew!)

This chapter covers various things you can do to recover:

82. Check the Pulse
83. Pinpoint the Problem
84. Recover: Take a Break
85. Recover: End Early
86. "Up" Your Energy Level
87. Get Up and Boogie
88. Lose the Notes
89. Step Out of the Spotlight: Involve the Group
90. Change Pace: Do Something Different
91. Pack Some Ideas Into Your Hip Pocket

"The worst thing is when the speaker stays on a predetermined track even when it's obvious that the audience is lost, bored, or leaving."

Attorney

82. Check the Pulse

You have approximately 2.5 minutes to assess the situation. Is it you, or is it them? If only one or two people are dozing off, and the remaining thirty-three are alert and interested, don't worry about it. Proceed. You might talk to the dozers during the break to check their interest levels, but you will not appeal to all listeners to the same degree. No problem. If, however, more than a few people are showing signs of boredom, then bail out and change course.

During one of my first presentations, I was delivering a lunchtime talk to about sixty members of the Rotary Club in rural Baldwin, Kansas. As I looked out into the audience, I noticed an elderly gentleman sleeping in the second row. I was devastated. I felt that my career was coming to an instant demise. Could my presentation really be so bad that someone would actually sleep through it? Luckily, the other fifty-nine people were attentive, eager listeners. My assessment? It was his problem, not mine. Prescription: Proceed!

A humor panel was delivering a breakout session at a national convention. After only five minutes, audience members began trailing out of the room until only about 25 percent of the original participants were left. The assessment? Speaker-related problems. Prescription: Bail out and change course. I left, too. The panel lacked preparation; they were obviously winging it; their attempts at humor were weak. One panel member was dominating the conversation. He did not use the mike correctly, and he could not be heard. The session was not going to be "how to," which was what the audience wanted. These panelists did not change their course, and suffered the consequences.

Bail-out idea: Wake up! Take charge of the situation before the participants leave. Stand up, involve the audience, and ask each person what he or she would like to accomplish in the session. Then do it!

83. Pinpoint the Problem

It's time to openly assess the situation. After all, things couldn't get much worse. What is the problem? Chances are, it is one of three things:

1. Your presentation
2. The audience
3. Logistics (warm room, pending company strike, tornado warnings)

Put your ego aside and be flexible for the good of the group. Find out what the problem is. Your dialog should go something like this:

"Seems like I'm getting off base, and I need your help to get me back on track. I'd like to stop and do a pulse check. That way, we can be sure that we're all headed in the right direction.

"How's the temperature in the room? Everybody comfortable?

"What do we need to do differently in order to get things rolling again?" (Brainstorm suggestions, break into small groups for discussion, or have people write down ideas and hand them forward. Include anything from topic content to comfort factors.)

"What are your top two or three priorities here? What do you need to know on this subject?

"What's the best way to proceed?" (Ask the audience for input.)

84. Recover: Take a Break

In my twenty years as a speaker and trainer, no one has ever complained about taking a break. It's one of my favorite escape routes when things are not going as planned. Audiences seem to enjoy taking a pause. It's a natural energizer. It also gives you a chance to collect your thoughts and regroup.

During the break, you can continue your investigation. Talk to some of the people in the audience. See if you can discover the true cause of the distress. It could be something logistical: The heat pump outside the window is too noisy; it's 4:30, and they thought you were ending at 4:00; there's a glare coming in from the window, and they can't see the TV monitor.

This is also a great opportunity to assess the interest level of individuals. Ask members of the audience questions such as: "Does this stuff make any sense to you?" "Are you learning anything?" "What would you like to do when we return from the break?"

Once the break has ended, you'll have a chance to recapture the audience. *Don't blow it! Change something now!* It's a new beginning. If you go back to the old routine, you've lost them. You have one chance to save yourself, and it's *now! Do something different!* The audience will forgive you for any previous offenses. But unless you correctly diagnose the problem *and solve it*, you'll return to the same old boring rut.

I was delivering team development training to a group of British Airways salespeople who had just consumed a monumental seven-course breakfast. After the first half-hour, I noticed that the group was extremely lethargic. I had them take a break, and during the break I devised a team-oriented activity that would take them outside the building—moving, walking, talking—for the next forty minutes. It was an instant success. Participation was full-blast. There was lots of activity, laughter, and enthusiasm. At the conclusion of the activity, they diagnosed their abilities and achievements on a team profile. It was a glowing recovery!

85. Recover: End Early

When you hit the doldrums and there's no quick fix in sight, you might consider ending early. It's certainly better than keeping your audience in "presentation prison." Sometimes it's the best option. Here's how to do it gracefully:

1. Announce that you will be ending early. (Immediately there will be a sigh of relief and a surge in the energy level.)
2. Tell them why you are ending early. Keep it positive. "I know I've packed a lot of information into this session. I think you've absorbed enough for one day, so let's call it a day. I'd like to finish with a few main points."
3. Summarize quickly—in five minutes or less. Do not violate your promise to end *now!*
4. WIFM: Explain what's in it for them.
5. GRABM: End with an attention-getter.

It was the second day of my Speakers Training Camp in Hood River, Oregon. All of the participants were preoccupied with the snow and ice storm that had occurred during the night. They were worried about getting to the airport safely and on time to catch their early evening flights. At the beginning of the day, I announced that I knew how concerned they were. In order to be sure that they traveled during the best possible time of day, I would end at 2:00 P.M. instead of the usual 5:00 P.M. I explained that the best time to make the 60-mile trek to the Portland airport was in midday, when the weather was warmest and the road crews had sanded the surface. I would still cover the major activities, and we would have a working lunch. From that point on, they gave me 100 percent of their attention. We covered all of the material, and everyone had a safe trip.

86. "Up" Your Energy Level

The audience sits out there like a bunch of chameleons. They will adapt to your mood. They will mirror you. If you are solemn and straight-faced, they will be solemn and straight-faced. If you are high-speed and jovial, they will be high-speed and jovial.

Check your personal energy level. Do you feel exhausted and lifeless? Does your voice sound monotone, uninteresting, and uninterested?

Maybe your style has become complacent and boring. Here are some ways to turn up the energy:

- ✓ Put more life into your voice. Get excited about your message.
- ✓ Smile!
- ✓ Magnify your facial expressions.
- ✓ Reactivate your eye contact (three- to five-second mini-conversations).
- ✓ Supercharge your gestures.
- ✓ Move around the room. Get closer to the audience.
- ✓ Vary the pace—sometimes fast, sometimes slow. Be unpredictable!

✓ Imagine that you are an actor. Act like a great speaker.
✓ Do something wild and wacky: scream, whisper, stand up on a chair, clap your hands, run around the room, pound your chest like King Kong.
✓ Use unusual character voices.

87. Get Up and Boogie

Get up. Get the energy flowing. Physical energy ignites mental energy. I attended a workshop with Anthony Robbins, the popular motivational expert. Anthony is an extremely high energy presenter. His ability to capture the audience is incredible. However, even though he had a very dynamic style, he knew that it would take more than that to hold the audience's attention during the three-hour afternoon portion of his program. That's a time when attention usually takes a major dip. What did he do? Every twenty minutes for the entire afternoon, he took a "back break." He asked everyone to stand, find a partner, and, depending on each person's comfort level, give that partner a vigorous back rub or "karate chops" on the back. The whole place erupted in laughter and movement. Best of all, it created a great energy boost—one that was repeated every twenty minutes.

One of my favorite energy boosters occurred after lunch at a convention I was attending at the Oregon coast. Again, the organizers knew the value of physical movement. Before the afternoon session, they had all the attendees assemble on a huge patio overlooking the bay. Then they taught everyone a country line dance. The music was blaring, 150 people were stepping in unison, and the sea lions were thoroughly entertained! It was a great release, and it paved the way for an afternoon of thinking and learning.

The responsibility for energy boosters can also be given to the participants. When faced with a warm training room one August day in Washington, D.C., I asked each of the participants to come up with a physical energizer. At intervals during the afternoon, one person was asked to conduct his or her activity. We marched; we did jumping jacks; we stampeded in place, we stretched; we did the "twist and shout"; we beat our chests and yelled "Tarzan." What fun!

88. Lose the Notes

Speakers who are glued to their notes are boring. They are relating to paper, not to people. Gather your guts and toss the notes. Reestablish your bond with the audience. This is really scary, but it might just be the way to save your presentation.

Think about carrying on a conversation with the audience. Suppose you were sitting across from someone having lunch, and you were discussing the topic. You'd know exactly what to say, and you wouldn't need notes. Treat the audience the same way. Don't worry about remembering every point; just hit the highlights. What are the two or three points you want them to remember? Be natural. Be conversational. Use examples. Engage the audience in discussion. Wing it. Then watch the audience's attention rise!

I was working with a phone company executive named Bob. He was a delightful person, full of laughter and enthusiasm. But when he delivered his presentation, he turned into a stilted, stone-faced figure, and the audience's attention flagged. Instead of talking to the audience, he was constantly looking at his notes, trying to read every word. On a scale of one to ten, his presentation ranked about a two. After he had finished, I took his notes away and asked him to deliver the presentation again. He turned three shades of blue. I gave the group a ten-minute break and told Bob to think of the three most important points in his presentation and "just tell us." He regained his composure, and did a 180-degree turnaround. He put his true lively personality into the presentation. He added some spontaneous stories and examples. He even included some off-the-cuff audience involvement. His three main points were emphasized very clearly. He was having fun, and the audience was having fun. Bob was a roaring success. In fact, when presentation 2 was over, the audience leaped to their feet, gave him a standing ovation, and broke into wild applause. The mist in our eyes said it all. Great recovery!

89. Step Out of the Spotlight: Involve the Group

Group involvement is usually a sure bet when you are trying to reactivate the interest level of your audience. It also takes the focus away from you and puts it back where it belongs: with the audience.

Divide the participants into groups of about five. Then use one of the following activities:

1. *Problem solution.* Considering the topic you are working on, ask the groups first to list the problems they see. Prioritize the problems. Then create some solutions to those problems. For example, if I were discussing the topic of nervousness, I would ask the groups to come up with a list of nervous symptoms that they have before giving a presentation. Then I would have them identify the most severe problems. Finally, I would ask them for some solutions to those problems. Groups usually will come up with 90 percent of the answers. It's your job to fill in the gaps as needed.

2. *Buzz groups.* Ask the people in each group to brainstorm lists of the following:

+ Questions
+ Comments
+ Ideas for applying this information to the job
+ Potential stumbling blocks

After ten minutes of discussion, each group presents its ideas to the others.

3. *Group presentations.* Write down the topics that need to be covered. Have each group select and discuss a topic, then and make a presentation on that topic.

90. Change Pace: Do Something Different

When you're in a rut, get out of it! And then never return to it. Think of changing the mood of the session:

✓ *Make physical changes.* Change groups, change chairs, go outside, change rooms, stand up, walk around, start a writing activity, have people huddle around a flip-chart activity. Put the group into a different physical environment. The more radical the change, the better.

✓ *Change speed.* If your pace has been slow, pick it up. If you have been in a high-energy mode, slow it down.

✓ *Change the activity.* If you are talking, start listening. If the focus is on you, put it back on the audience. If you are lecturing, change to group participation. If you are involved in a large-group discussion, change it to small-group discussion. If you have been working in groups of five, mix up the groups—add some new faces to each team. Change the team leaders.

✓ *Have a snack break.* Perhaps the group is starting to run out of fuel, especially in the afternoon. I was conducting a two-day workshop in Tampa for a group of trainers. They were extremely eager and interested participants in the morning, but in the afternoon, I noticed a sudden decline in energy level. I really felt that the activities were fun and on target, but for some reason, this group was having a real attention dip. I changed activities, changed the pace of the session, and tried every trick in the book. About that time, my stomach started to growl. Was that the secret? Was this group hungry? There was a pop machine, but no snacks had been provided by their company for the afternoon session. The second day, I came in with healthy energy boosters for the afternoon: fig bars, pretzels, popcorn. An amazing thing happened: great energy all afternoon!

91. Pack Some Ideas Into Your Hip Pocket

When I was an undergraduate at Penn State University, my Speech 101 professor often told the class, "Always have something in your hip pocket." He explained that since you can't predict what's going to happen during every moment of a presentation, you should have a plan for expanding or shrinking your talk. Also, have at least five ideas to perk up your presentation if the attention level sags.

Here's a guideline: Be able to add to or shrink your talk by 25 percent. That way, you will have already thought out ways to condense or expand the topic if you need to. For example, for my two-day Speakers Training Camp, I have at least three hours of additional material and activities that I can adapt to the group on the spot. Many of these activities are written out and categorized on index cards, so that they are readily accessible. In almost every session, I pull out some of my "hip-pocket" ideas. One morning, the participants asked for some fun and innovative ideas to use during routine review of training material. I had the group brainstorm some ideas, and then I told them that one of my favorite activities for review was a Jeopardy game. Many of them were not familiar with the format for using the game in a large group, and asked for a demonstration. Luckily, it was one of my hip-pocket ideas, and I could conduct the game on the spot. All of the game questions related to the topic of presentation skills. The group thoroughly enjoyed the activity, and were amazed that I could pull off such a feat at a moment's notice. I explained to them the value of my hip pockets! (Actual preparation time for the questions used in the game was about two hours.)

Here are some universal ideas to fill your pockets: group activities, newspaper articles, aha sheets (participants write down the two most important things they've learned), prizes, action plans, pictures (attendees draw pictures of what they've learned), games (that relate to the topic), discussion topics, role play, "What would you do if . . . ," case studies.

Chapter 10

Stupid Meetings?
Try Some Steak, Sizzle,
and Style

Most meetings stink. They reek of poor organization and indecision. Worst of all, they are boring time wasters.

In the five zillion meetings taking place in the United States right now, how many participants do you think are really happy to be there? How many do you think would prefer an emergency call on their pager? Managers tell me that meetings are the number-1 cause of unproductive time—even outweighing complaints about paperwork, mail, phone calls, and travel.

You've seen how the steak, sizzle, and style techniques apply to presentations. In this chapter, those concepts will be applied to another type of presentation challenge: conducting creative and productive meetings.

92. Say "No" to Meetings
93. Meeting Steak: Cut the Fat
94. Keep It Quick and Snappy: Twenty-Five Steps to a Fifty-Nine-Minute Meeting
95. Keep on Track With the Fifty-Nine-Minute Meeting Guide
96. Gather Your Guts: Evaluate Your Meeting
97. Have Fun! Add Meeting Sizzle
98. Assign a Cast of Characters
99. Become a Fantastic Facilitator
100. Waltz Through Sticky Situations
101. Rate Your Meeting Style

> *"A meeting leader needs to be a bright spot of intelligence—a person that gives the group direction . . . a forward thinker . . . one who is perfectly at ease and in authority."*
>
> —Manager, Advanced Training Technologies

92. Say No to Meetings

The best meeting is the one that never happens. In fact, 90 percent of the time, there's a better, quicker way to get the job done. Someone once said that meetings are called by managers who get lonely. When you're thinking about having a meeting, think again. It seems as though the more successful you are in the organization, and the jazzier your title is, the more time you spend in meetings. It's time to take a giant "whoa."

There's only one good reason for having a meeting: to develop and promote team spirit within your organization.

Ask these questions when you are thinking about scheduling a meeting:

- ✦ What is my objective in having a meeting?
- ✦ Is there a quicker, better way to accomplish this objective?
- ✦ Will this meeting utilize the team and promote team spirit?
- ✦ What is the worst thing that could happen if we don't have a meeting?

After answering the questions above, pick one of these alternatives. Be a meeting cop. See the stop sign, then choose a different route 90 percent of the time!

Meeting Alternatives:

Memo	Delegating assignments
Hallway discussion	Company newsletter
Phone call	Questionnaire

Conference call   Suggestion box
Fax   Bulletin board
Electronic mail   Project teams

93. Meeting Steak: Cut the Fat

So you've pondered the alternatives, you've decided that a meeting would help to develop and promote your group's team
spirit, and you've come to the conclusion that a meeting is
indeed a true and honest necessity. It's the best way to accomplish your objectives. Then it's time to take the meeting leader's
pledge.

Meeting Leader's Pledge

 I promise to stay out of the depths of Meeting Hell. From
this day forward, I will hold 50 percent fewer meetings. No
meeting shall last longer than fifty-nine minutes. I will have
a clear and simple agenda. I will keep the meeting focused. I
will invite only those people whose attendance is absolutely
necessary. I will do my homework before the meeting and
send out an agenda. I will start and end the meeting on
time. I will use visual aids to keep the meeting moving. I
will become an expert facilitator, helping each person to
contribute to the meeting objectives in an efficient and positive way. I will be sure that each person in attendance has
an opportunity to speak at each meeting. I will help the
group focus on solving problems and creating action items.
I will do my homework after the meeting and follow up on
action items. And when the meeting is over and all of the
troops go home, I will ask myself this simple question:
"Was it worth it?"

---

94. Keep It Quick and Snappy: Twenty-Five Steps to a Fifty-Nine–Minute Meeting

Pre-Meeting

1. Write down the objectives, expectations, and desired
   outcomes. What question should the meeting answer?
   Write it down.

2. Why have a meeting? Is there a better alternative?
3. Who absolutely positively needs to be there? (Remember that everyone should contribute.)
4. When should the meeting be held?
5. Where should the meeting be held? What is the best room arrangement?
6. How many people will be attending?
7. Determine the process for conducting the meeting (short presentations, question and answer, brainstorming, small group discussion).
8. Set a time limit.
9. Prepare an agenda and write down a time limit for each item.
10. Distribute the agenda before the meeting.
11. Arrive early. Set up the meeting room. Claim the head of the table.

The Meeting

12. Start on time—no matter what!
13. Make introductions (quickly).
14. Review the agenda, objectives, expectations, and the question to be answered by the end of the meeting.
15. Announce the time limits and post the agenda (with time limits indicated). Pace the meeting to the agenda. Assign a timekeeper to monitor the time.
16. Focus the group on the issues. Include input from everyone.
17. Use visual aids to stress a point.

Wrap Up

18. Summarize. Answer the question posed at the beginning of the meeting.
19. Identify action items. Who? What? By when? Write them down.
20. Arrange for follow-up.
21. Make a closing statement. End on time, no matter what!

Post-Meeting

22. Evaluate the meeting. Have the participants complete written critiques occasionally. Welcome the feedback.

23. Prepare a memo and send a copy of action items to participants.
24. Follow up on action items.
25. Whew! Are you sure there isn't a quicker, better alternative to having a meeting?

95. Keep on Track With the Fifty-Nine-Minute Meeting Guide

The fifty-nine-minute guide is shown in Figure 10-1. The plan and agenda sections should be filled out prior to the meeting and sent to each attendee. List the action items during the final stage of the meeting. After the meeting, give each attendee a copy of the action items.

96. Gather Your Guts: Evaluate Your Meeting

You'll never know how effective your meetings are unless you ask. Don't let your position get in the way of reality. Gather your guts and ask how the meeting is going. You can do this with a five-minute discussion at the end of the meeting, or you can hand out feedback forms to the participants—to be filled out before the meeting is over. Have the evaluations done immediately. If you ask that the forms be filled out and returned later, you'll rarely get them all back.

Here are some questions you can ask:

- ✓ Did we achieve our meeting objectives as indicated in the agenda?
- ✓ What two things did you like best about this meeting?
- ✓ What are two things that could be improved next time?
- ✓ What can the meeting leader do to improve the meeting?
- ✓ What can the participants do to improve the meeting?
- ✓ Was this meeting really necessary? Was it worth the time?
- ✓ What is a better alternative to a meeting?
- ✓ Other suggestions?

Figure 10-1. Fifty-nine-minute meeting guide.

Meeting: Date:

Called by: Start Time:

Participants: End Time:

Objectives: 1.   Place:

          2.   Please Bring:

          3.

          4.

What question should be answered?

Agenda

Agenda Items	Person Responsible	Time
1.		
2.		
3.		
4.		
5.		
6.		

Action Items

Who	What	When
1.		
2.		
3.		
4.		
5.		

Sometimes it is helpful to conduct a mid-meeting pulse check. If you sense that you are "bombing," take action right away. Participants generally welcome the opportunity to get things back on track.

What do you do when you are a meeting participant and the leader is not conducting the meeting in an organized way? Speak up! The group will thank you for it. Think "focus" and "action." You might say something like this: "We're getting way off track here. Let's focus back on the issue: Where should we put our extra advertising dollars? Let's list some possibilities on the flip chart."

97. Have Fun! Add Meeting Sizzle

Beware: If you arrive late at one of Art Clark's meetings, he'll make you stand up and sing an entire song. Art is a senior vice president at Boat/U.S. in Alexandria, Virginia. He's famous for putting fun and energy into his meetings. By the way, people rarely show up late! Here are some ways to add to the fun factor:

+ Reward people for coming on time. Bite-size candy bars, stickers, and small tokens are great for this.
+ Admonish people (in a humorous way) for arriving late. One manager uses an inexpensive flushing-toilet bank. If you come in late, you have to put a quarter in the toilet and flush it! The sound is very realistic and is a funny announcement that you're late.
+ Establish a policy of fining people if the meeting goes overtime. One group fines everyone ten cents per minute of overtime. The leader is fined a dollar per minute.
+ Use a funny timing device, such as a honking horn or a talking doll, when it's time to move on to the next topic.
+ Use koosh balls to throw at meeting offenders: time wasters, sidetrackers, or people who fall asleep.
+ Have a stand-up meeting: no cushy chairs, no food, no coffee. These combat conditions ensure quick progress.
+ If there is a lull in the action, get the blood flowing again. Have the participants stand up and do ten jumping jacks.

✦ Give each person a few participation tickets. When a person contributes to the meeting, one of his or her tickets goes into a basket. Draw for a prize at the end of the meeting.

98. Assign a Cast of Characters

Have fun and increase involvement by distributing some of the meeting responsibilities.

✦ *Timekeeper.* This individual is critical to the success of the meeting. Assign this job to someone who is overly verbal at meetings. It will help this person condense his or her thoughts. Remember to use an unusual timing signal, such as a honking horn, a bell, or a mooing cow toy. It's also the job of the timekeeper to be sure that the meeting starts and ends on time.

✦ *Maestro.* Choose a person who is an excellent observer and facilitator. This person is in charge of meeting harmony— the process of getting things done. It's best to establish a list of meeting guidelines and post them. When one of the guidelines is being violated (and the meeting leader doesn't do anything about it), the maestro speaks up and gets things moving again. Some guidelines might include:

Meeting Guidelines
✓ Stay focused on the agenda.
✓ Be positive and action-oriented.
✓ Don't dominate the discussion.
✓ Discuss issues, not personalities.

✦ *Recorder.* This is an unpopular but necessary role. People generally do not enjoy being the meeting secretary. The recorder writes down important information, especially the action items.

✦ *Scorekeeper.* The scorekeeper is in charge of collecting feedback on the meeting. This can be done in writing or verbally. What went right? What went wrong? Keep it short and simple.

99. Become a Fantastic Facilitator

Meetings that sizzle need a strong leader, one who can ignite group interaction. Here's how:

- ✓ Remember that you are a facilitator, not a participant. It is your job to involve the group and move their ideas toward positive action. Let them come up with the ideas and the solutions.
- ✓ Your best weapon is the pause. When you ask a question or seek a response from the group, count to twenty in your head. It will seem like forever, but it takes about twenty seconds for ideas to kick in. Good facilitators become masters of the pause.
- ✓ Let the participants feel free to discover and make mistakes. Hold back. Let them come up with the answers. Fight off the urge to have the last say.
- ✓ If someone has a question or concern, ask the whole group for reactions.
- ✓ Be an example of enthusiasm and energy. Be interested in the participants. Be curious! Be positive! The group members will emulate you.
- ✓ Listen! Listen! Listen!
- ✓ Listen with your eyes as well as with your ears. Look for signals of disinterest, confusion, excitement. Adapt as needed.
- ✓ If you are recording information on a flip chart, write down exactly what is said. Abbreviations are fine, but use the participants' words, not yours. For example, if someone says "personality indicators," don't change it to "personality styles." There's something psychological about this. When the words are recorded exactly as they were spoken, the contributor feels as though the leader is truly listening and understands the message. If the words are changed, it seems as though the leader is guiding the meeting toward his or her own objectives.
- ✓ Be flexible, even if it means killing the original agenda. Keep the ball rolling.
- ✓ Have fun!

If the goal of the meeting is to solve a problem, follow these seven easy steps.

Facilitator's Guide to Solving a Problem

1. Define the problem. Write it on a flip chart or transparency. Be sure that everyone understands the problem.
2. Brainstorm solutions to the problem. Go around the room and obtain feedback from each person. If someone doesn't have an idea to contribute, it's OK to say "pass." This method gets everyone involved. Write down the possible solutions.
3. Discuss possible solutions.
4. Select a solution.
5. Write down an action plan.
6. Implement the action plan.
7. Evaluate the success of the plan.

Group involvement in meetings is not a quick process. However, it accomplishes the objectives of promoting team spirit and spreading responsibility for problem solving to the team. When people suggest solutions to problems, they have a tendency to buy into the change.

When I was the Quality Circles (problem-solving) facilitator at General Dynamics in San Diego, I was in charge of a team of machinists who needed to solve some problems. Solving just one problem required about five one-hour meetings. However, the pride and camaraderie that developed within the group was well worth the time and effort.

100. Waltz Through Sticky Situations

Perfect meetings are about as common as gray palominos. Things happen; agendas go awry; attendees will throw you a curve. Put these ideas into your hip pocket, and you'll become the Arthur Murray of the meeting world.

Sticky Situation 1: It's time for discussion, and no one has anything to say.

Don't panic. Remember that most folks have been trained to take directions. Many do not know how to take an active part in decision making.

Encourage comments:	"Harry, what do you think?" "Let's go around the room. I'd like to get everyone's reaction." "Linda, what would you do in this situation?"
Write down ideas:	"I'd like everyone to get out a piece of paper and write down three possibilities."

Sticky Situation 2: Someone is dominating the session.

Equalize involvement:	"Just a minute, Bob; let's hear from some of the others." "Tom, what do you think?"

Sticky Situation 3: There's lots of discussion, but no decisive action.

Survey the group:	"Can we have a quick show of hands? How many think this would work?" "We'll go around the room and let everyone voice an opinion on this."
Discuss possibilities:	"Let's list some possibilities."
Imagine outcomes:	"Imagine that you are the customer. How would you react to this?" "Imagine that we go ahead with this idea. What would the situation look like in a month?"

Write a plan:	"Let's formulate an action plan on the flip chart." "Joan, can you start us off?"

Sticky Situation 4: People are arguing a point. They're divided on an issue. No progress is being made.

Clarify the objective or the problem	"Time out. We need to take a pause in the action and focus back on the objective/problem."
Turn opinions into positive suggestions:	"We've had enough time to air our opinions. It's time to turn those opinions into solutions. First, state your opinion in one sentence; then suggest something positive we can do about the situation."
Combine needs/ prioritize:	"We have lots of different concerns and suggestions here. We need to prioritize these and come up with a plan we can live with."
Other options:	Take a break. Table the issue. Do some fact-finding. Turn it over to a committee for recommendations.

101. Rate Your Meeting Style

Instructions: Check yes or no for each of the following. These items are based on what audiences like most about a presenter's style. Be honest.

YES   NO

_____ _____   1. Am I enthusiastic about running meetings?

_____ _____   2. Am I a confident leader? Do I establish

YES   NO

an agenda, guide participants through it, and conclude with action items?

_____ _____ 3. Do I work at being dynamic, lively, energetic? Do I smile and use steady eye contact and gestures to convey my message?

_____ _____ 4. Am I sincere? Do I really believe in the group process? Am I a facilitator rather than a dictator?

_____ _____ 5. Do I use a strong and commanding voice? Do I speak with conviction?

_____ _____ 6. Am I a passionate person? Do I really strive to get things done? Do I really care about this group and its goals?

_____ _____ 7. Do I speak with lots of voice energy? Do I change volume and pitch and use pauses in order to make my voice more interesting?

_____ _____ 8. Do I use visual aids to keep things on track and to record participant ideas?

_____ _____ 9. Am I an expert listener?

_____ _____ 10. Do I welcome ideas, controversy, and opposing views?

Chapter 11
This Stuff Really Works

I had just completed the manuscript for this book, and I decided to take a break. I was reading the local newspaper when I noticed the headline: "High School Students Hear Motivational Talk." I couldn't help but think, "That poor speaker dude trying to impress a bunch of high school kids. Good luck!" I read the article. It was 10:00 A.M.; the talk was going to start at 12:15. I couldn't miss this opportunity. I've appeared before appliance parts salespeople, accountants, and even butchers, but the thought of going before a group of high school kids would give me the willies. I couldn't wait to observe the "motivational speaker" trying to motivate a group of teens. I thought that this had to be the toughest audience in the world.

The local high school was only about four miles away. I arrived early so I that could watch the audience enter the gym. Just as I thought: they were giggling, noisy, shouting, shuffling, and slow to take their seats. This was one tough audience. I was so happy that I wasn't the speaker.

What I discovered that day surprised me. It shouldn't have, because it's everything this book is about. What I found was a "10"—a speaker so good that he captivated a gymnasium full of teenagers for one hour and twenty minutes. How did he do it? He did everything I've described in this book: steak, sizzle, and style. What excited me was seeing all of it put into action in front of these kids. This stuff really works! I've seen it work for years in front of adult audiences, but to see it work in this crowd really convinced me that these techniques produce phenomenal results.

The speaker was Mark Scharenbroich from Minneapolis. He

was a freelance speaker sponsored by Jostens, the company famous for its high school rings. Mark was one of those speakers who was fun and funny, and he had a very strong message. I feverishly took notes so that I could tell you about some of the things he did and said.

Steak: Here are just a few of the thoughts he conveyed:

+ Think about sharing instead of comparing.
+ Choose life over existence.
+ No risks, no rewards.
+ Be a better friend to your friends.
+ Find out what you're good at and be good at it.
+ Be like a baby. Kiss yourself in the mirror. Get excited. Babies don't start gangs because the others are wearing the wrong color of Pampers that day.

He spoke the language of the students: OK, OK, OK, all right, shut up, cool, humongous.

Sizzle: He used simple props: a student's desk at one end of the gym, and a music stand. Often he would sit at the desk and pretend to be a student, raising his hand wildly or slumping in his seat. He used gold stars with the theme "above and beyond," and gave out a few to students.

He told lots of personal stories. One was about his Catholic school experience: "Our Father, who art in heaven, how do you know my name?"

The students really laughed during his story about being a lineman on the high school team. He referred to the line as "the wall," and the quarterback was "the princess dancing behind the wall."

Mark used a lot of audience involvement. He had the kids raise their hands from time to time in response to his questions. He had a few students participate in various segments of his talk. He teased some of the teachers—to the delight of the students!

He used participation in the grand finale. He stood at the music stand and conducted students on each side of the gym in a roaring series of chants: "boom-ba" (on one side); "hey!" (on the other side). It was an uplifting way to end the session.

Author's note: Mark used sizzle at least once every two minutes. I noticed that if he spoke for more than two minutes with just straight talk, the students became a little restless, and then pow! He'd give them another dose of sizzle to hold their interest. With adults, you need sizzle once every six minutes. You can see that there's a need for more sizzle, more often with the younger crowd.

Style: Mark's gestures were huge. He walked, ran, shuffled, and stood all over that gym floor. His arms exaggerated the movements: driving a car, passing a football, toddling like a baby. It was an enormous space, and he did a terrific job of moving throughout that space.

His eye contact was riveting. He stopped and looked eyeball to eyeball right at the students in various sections of the gym. If a certain group became noisy or listless, he would move to that area quickly and look right at the kids.

Mark went beyond his normal personality. He was an actor. He was a ham. He had a big message, and he delivered it in a big way.

His voice hit every possible note. He sounded out the characters' voices in his stories: a first grader's enthusiasm, a freshman's fear, a teacher's commands, a baby's silliness.

How he related: The kids liked Mark because he spoke on their terms. Right at the beginning of his talk, he put himself in their shoes. He said, "You're probably wondering, 'So, Mr. speaker guy—what kind of advice do you have for us during this magical time of our life . . . ?'" He said that he was not going to make a motivational speech. In order to make a motivational speech, "you kind of have to be yippy zippy." He added that he wouldn't be talking about drugs and death stats. You could feel a sigh of relief penetrating the room. Mark then added, "If you can't motivate yourself, how do you think I can?" This was the best thing he could have done. Now the students knew he was not going to try to motivate them to do anything, and they were willing to listen.

He joked with the freshmen, with the sophomores, with the juniors, and with the seniors. Everyone knew that he had walked in their shoes at one time.

His last name was difficult to pronounce, and he made fun of it. His name is Scharenbroich, but he told the kids just to call him "Shake 'n Bake."

He had done his homework. He knew about the losses of the struggling boys' basketball team; he knew that the school's choir was headed for state competition for the eleventh straight year; he knew about the school's mascot.

What fun I had that day seeing all of this occur just down the road at the local high school. It was the ultimate test of steak, sizzle, and style. Next to these kids, business audiences are a breeze.

Dissecting speakers is one of my favorite ways to expand my own skills. I like to take presentations apart bit by bit. I want to see what the speakers do, and how they do it. I encourage you to do the same. See what you like. Have you noticed anything that you'd like to try in your own presentations? What are some things that you didn't like? Remember to avoid those pitfalls.

I want to encourage you to keep trying out new ideas. I've been doing the Speakers Training Camp for almost ten years, and it's always changing. I've never done the same program twice. There's always a new story, a new prop, a new audience challenge. Have fun with presentations. Your audience will thank you for it!

Conclusion

That's it, the pot of gold. You're ready to captivate any business audience. It's all about steak, sizzle, and style. And the guts to go for it! Good luck. And have fun.

Part Four

Standing Ovation: Quick Tips and Resources

Camp Chat: Answers to the Most Frequently Asked Questions

For the last year, I have kept track of the questions asked by participants in the Speakers Training Camp. The following questions seem to crop up at every session. I hope the answers will clarify any remaining concerns you may have. If you have additional questions, please send them to me, Sue Gaulke, in care of AMACOM Books, 1601 Broadway, New York, NY 10019.

I still feel awkward with gestures. What do I do with my hands and arms?

This is a very popular question, and it always pops up after our first videotaping of participants. The goal is to have natural, free-flowing gestures. Restricted hands and elbows glued to your side will diminish your power. The more space you take up, the more powerful you'll appear. Most gestures should be about waist high with your armpits out. Increase the size and range of gestures for more emphasis and for larger groups. The best rule of thumb is, don't let your hands touch—they usually get into trouble, or become stuck in a position such as the "fig leaf." If you find that your hands do become stuck in something like a "Hail Mary" position (prayer position), let your arms and hands hang loosely by your side. This is the best neutral position. In everyday conversation, you don't think about your gestures. You let them happen naturally. Do the same in your presentations.

How can I overcome the fear?

First, keep things in perspective. You know more about your topic than anyone else in the room. Believe it!

Next, be yourself. Let your personality emerge. Being natural and warm is much better than being perfect. The audience accepts goofs, blunders, and mistakes. They recognize that you are human. However, they will not accept nervous and distracting mannerisms.

Fill your head with positive thoughts, even if you have to force them. I am a great believer in positive thinking. Visualizing and rehearsing a successful presentation in your mind will strengthen your comfort level with the material. It will also transfer to your audience.

Be prepared. Practice your presentation six times, with your audiovisuals, and it will seem as though you have really internalized it. Try using audio or video recordings to check your progress.

Breathe! Practice both deep breathing and positive thinking on a daily basis—not just five minutes before a presentation.

The most important tip is to have fun. If you are having fun, chances are, so is your audience.

If I feel that I'm bombing or the audience isn't paying attention, what can I do?

Change. Right now! Here are your best options:

1. Switch gears and open it up for questions or discussion, then focus on the areas of greatest interest.
2. Ask the audience what they need to know on your topic. You can obtain this information through oral or written responses.
3. Break into small groups. This works well and activates the audience's thinking.
4. Add more sizzle to your presentation. Stories and examples will usually wake up a crowd.
5. End early. Sometimes this is your best option.

It's helpful to actually have a few ideas in mind in case this happens.

When I'm giving a presentation, should I change my natural, everyday self?

Yes and no. Let your personality shine through. Audiences are looking for personable, memorable characters. Let it rip! I'm always reminding my Speakers Training Camp attendees to take 100 percent of their personality up in front of the group. Some personalities, however, need more than 100 percent. They are not exciting enough to captivate the audience for any length of time. If this is true of you, you can enhance your natural style by adding more voice variety, movement, energy, pause, facial expression, super eye contact. These skills can be learned, even though they may not be a part of your natural repertoire. Be yourself, then ham it up as needed. Remember, above all else, the audience is looking for lots of enthusiasm!

How can I rivet the audience?

According to audience research, keep focused on three main areas. These are the overwhelming favorites among audiences across the country:

1. *Steak:* A simple, memorable message, well organized, and cooked to order for each particular audience.
2. *Sizzle:* Make the talk interesting, using stories, personal anecdotes, examples, and humor. Add sizzle every six minutes.
3. *Style:* Audiences like enthusiasm. Use lots of voice energy, facial expression, and gestures. Move!

Surprise them occasionally. Do the unexpected. This will help the audience to remember you and your presentation.

How can I be sure that the audience is understanding my message?

First, be sure that your message can be boiled down into one simple, clear sentence. Repeat your message at least six times during your presentation. Check the audience's understanding by having them repeat the message back to you.

If you are questioning the audience's understanding of a particular section of your presentation, ask them, "What points do I need to clear up here? Where do we need to spend more time? Are you ready to move on?" If your topic is a lengthy one, you can use mini-summaries at the end of each major section. In addition, handouts will reinforce your message.

What are the best ways to prepare?

Each person has his or her own preparation ritual. I have just one giant Don't: DO NOT WRITE OUT YOUR PRESENTATION WORD FOR WORD. Audiences do not want you to read your presentation. Here's a quick and simple method of preparation:

- ✓ Do a five-minute idea web. Blast as many ideas onto the page as you possibly can. Let your thoughts flow.
- ✓ Complete an audience profile. Find out as much as you can about the audience.
- ✓ Select three to five main topics. Remember to keep it simple.
- ✓ Break down the original topics into subtopics. The longer your presentation, the more subtopics.
- ✓ Simplify your message into one sentence.
- ✓ Add sizzle every 6 minutes to maintain audience attention.
- ✓ Prepare simple, clear visual aids.
- ✓ Practice your presentation several times from start to finish. Practice with your visual aids, too. Think about enthusiasm, energy, eye contact, smiling, gestures, and voice.
- ✓ Visualize yourself doing a great job. Visualize your audience enjoying your presentation.
- ✓ Keep breathing—deep breathing!

What are the best ways to practice?

Run through your presentation from start to finish, using your actual notes and visual aids. Scatter some chairs in a room, and put some stuffed animals or dolls on them. This is a great way to practice eye contact. Use a timer or stopwatch to estimate time. If possible, record yourself with a video camera or audio recorder. If you're using a video camera, you can put the camera on a tripod and let the tape roll. You don't need anyone in the room to operate it. After you've gone through your presentation once, critique yourself. Complete the **Master Checklist** on page 148 as you review the tape.

Even if you do not have access to a video or audio recorder, practice is helpful. It will give you a feeling for the flow and timing of your material. Some people like to practice in front of a mirror. That's fine; it's a matter of personal choice.

How can I answer questions confidently?

After you've prepared your material, write down the twenty questions that the audience is most likely to ask. Be prepared to answer them. This may surprise you, but you will have figured out at least 90 percent of the questions.

Before you answer a question, clarify it if necessary. If you're in a large group, repeat it so that the entire audience can hear it. Also, make a quick judgment call. Is this question one person's isolated concern, or is it something of interest to the entire group? You can always turn the question back to the group and let them express their viewpoint.

Answer the question simply and to the point. Add one example or one piece of supporting information and then stop. Do not give a mini-lecture. Another way to handle questions is to have people write their concerns on an "issues chart" in the room. That way, you can deal with these issues at the appropriate point in the program.

Can I use notes?

Yes! Absolutely! It is not necessary to memorize your material. The goal here is to use inconspicuous notes like these:

use large printing

lots of space

yellow lined paper (great!)

medium flare pen

2–3 words/line

With large, simple notes, you'll be able to see them from about six feet away. The audience does not mind if you use notes. It's how you handle them that counts. If you keep your notes large and simple, you can glance at them to scoop up your idea, then deliver your message with your eyes up and focused on the audience. The audience wants your focus on them, not on your notes for extended periods of time. Another tip is to staple a few pages of notes together. If you use a single sheet of paper, it will rattle and shake if you are nervous. I do not like index cards for recording notes. Flipping the cards during the actual presentation seems too mechanical.

It's OK to hold your notes. Continue to gesture, primarily with the opposite hand. When you are not using the notes, set them down.

How can I remind myself to work on a particular skill (such as eye contact or enthusiasm) while I am actually making a presentation?

Develop a reminder system. You can write words in the margin of your notes in bright colors: SMILE!, EYE CONTACT!, ARMS! If you're using transparencies, put reminder sheets between the transparencies. Another idea is to have a buddy in the audience who can give you an inconspicuous signal as needed. Give yourself some feedback after the presentation.

My company is relaxing its dress code. How do I dress for success in my presentations?

There are several considerations:

+ Dress one notch better than the best-dressed person in the room. First impressions are important. Dressing up is safer than dressing down.
+ Dress *only* in what makes you look good. For example, if you're a woman and you look better in skirts than pants, stick with the skirts.
+ Wear colors with powerful impact: blue, black, gray, white, burgundy, red.
+ Use contrast between layers, such as a very light shirt or blouse with a dark jacket or sweater.

- Accessorize with a tie or bold jewelry.
- Buy the best quality you can afford.
- Consider your role in the organization.
- Consider the expectations of the audience.
- Stay away from fads and distractions, such as dangling earrings.

How can I make my ideas stick?

Be sure that you have a clear and simple message—one word, one phrase, or one sentence. Repeat that message at least six times during your presentation. Use some sizzle, like a story, metaphor, or magic trick. Reinforce your message visually through the use of visual aids, handouts, or give-aways (pens, badges, desk signs). If possible, have the audience internalize the message by saying it out loud, writing it down, describing what they will do with the information. Plan a follow-up to check retention and accomplishments.

How can I become a memorable, one-of-a-kind presenter?

You need to discover or devise a certain uniqueness. This could involve the way you look, the way you act, or the way you sound. It could be a hobby or gimmick that you weave into your presentations. It could be an unusual personal title, such as "The Time Wizard." Or your presentation could have an outstanding theme, title, or message.

Some speakers are famous for a particular type of sizzle, such as their stories, magic tricks, or audience interaction. You need to figure out what makes you different from everyone else. Pick a style you are comfortable with, and one you can call your own.

How do you expand a half-hour talk into a three-hour talk?

Remember that the body of your talk is like a chest of drawers. In each drawer, you put one main topic. Rather than adding more main topics, consider going into more depth with the ideas that you already have. In other words, put more stuff in each drawer. Also add more sizzle—audience involvement, examples, humor.

How can I be sure that I am interesting?

First, be sure that your style sparkles: smile, use good eye contact, use gestures, move around, put some oomph into your voice. Be enthusiastic! Then use some sizzle every six minutes. Observe the audience. If the people look bored, try some group participation, take a break, or summarize and end early. You can always obtain written or verbal feedback midway through or at the end of your talk.

How can I develop rapport with the audience?

Do your homework. Find out as much as you can about the audience. Read their local paper, the company newsletter, and their industry magazine. Then talk about things that relate to their world: their community, their sports teams, their hobbies, their interests, their industry. Talk to some of the people before the session. Make some friends. Know some of their names, and use their names in your presentation. Check your body language. Be sure that you look friendly—smile, use great eye contact, and sound enthusiastic about being there!

I have trouble staying on track. How can I be sure that my main points are covered?

Rely on visual aids to keep you on track. Have your main points written on transparencies, slides, or a flip chart. Then use those aids as you progress through your talk. End your talk with a crisp, clear summary that ties your points together.

How can I do a better job of thinking on my feet?

This is a tough one. Some people are better at this than others. First, be an expert in your subject. The more you know, the more confident you will feel about ad-libbing. Second, be flexible. Don't lock yourself into a rigid outline. Some of the best material includes spontaneous stories and remarks. Think of your presentation as carrying on a conversation with your audience. People rarely are at a loss for words when they are in the midst of a conversation.

If you don't know the answer to a question, admit it. Then turn it over to the group for comments and discussion.

I am petrified in front of a group. How can I find more enjoyment in giving presentations?

Keep things in perspective. Chances are, your presentation will not make the news that day. It's not as important as you think! Often we blow things out of proportion. Keep your message simple. Prepare your visual aids ahead of time, and let them guide you through your thoughts. Put some personal interest into the presentation, something that delights you: a story about your vacation, a golf tournament, your champion ten-year-old pitching star. Meet a few people in the audience before the program. It's comforting to know that you have a few friends out there. Finally, concentrate on the audience and what they'll get out of your presentation. Take the focus off of yourself and your own inhibitions. Have fun!

I feel comfortable in front of a small group, but I'm worried about appearing in front of several hundred people. Any tips?

Think conversation. You're merely having a chat with a few more people. It's a mind game that you play with yourself. Everything needs to be bigger—your visual aids need larger print, your gestures need to be larger, your voice should be a bit more dramatic, your eye contact needs to reach out to all areas of the room. But for the most part, you can do just about anything with a large group that you can do with a smaller one. Audience participation activities can be adapted. Be creative. If you want maximum audience interaction, seat the people at round tables. Your space in front of a large group is also very important to your own comfort level. I would feel like a caged beast behind a podium. I use a table to my right to hold notes, props, a small clock, and a glass of water. This is the same setup that I use for small groups.

How do you pace and time your presentation?

During your practice, you can time the various sections of your presentation. Remember that the actual presentation usually will take a little longer. Be sure to allow time for audience participation and questions. Write down some approximate time guidelines in the margins of your notes. Always plan out what you will do if you need to fill up some additional time—have a few topics and audience interaction activities on hand, just in case you need them. Don't worry about ending early. The audience will thank you. You can put a clock with large numbers near your notes to guide you. It's much better than constantly glancing at your watch.

How do you prepare for an audience in which there are different levels of knowledge about your subject?

You do what newspapers do: Strike a balance by targeting the average listener. Be sure to define any terms that might not be understood by all. You can appeal to the upper level in the group through the examples, stories, and question-and-answer sessions. Remember that you can also utilize handout material that covers both basic and advanced concepts. It's also helpful to admit to the audience that you know that there are various ability levels, and that you will try to present something of interest to everyone.

I have a really boring voice. How can I practice voice fluctuations?

Use a tape recorder, listen to your own voice. Practice exaggerating your voice. Pretend that you are an actor or actress. Tape yourself while reading a paragraph in your normal voice. Then read the paragraph in a very loud and mean voice. Read it in a soft and wise voice. Read it in a wild and silly voice. Keep practicing different characters and different voices. Really exaggerate. Then, when you practice your presentation, go overboard with your voice: louder, softer, faster, slower, higher, lower, pause. Tape yourself again and listen. By working with the extremes, you will learn the skills of voice change. If you're still having trouble, you can contact a speech pathologist in your area for assistance.

How do I decide on the right visuals to use for different audiences?

There are four things to consider. First, how many people are in the audience? Be sure that your visuals can be seen by all. Second, consider what type of visual aid will work best for the message. A full-color slide show is very appealing, but transparencies are very convenient for spontaneous writing. Third, take into consideration the visual aids generally used by your audience. When I worked for General Dynamics, everyone used overhead projectors and transparencies. In that environment, a flip-chart presentation would not have carried the same amount of credibility. The fourth consideration is you. What types of audiovisual aids do you prefer? I love flip charts! They're so calm and natural and low-tech. When I use flip charts, I am at my best. Another thought: you can always use a few different types of audiovisuals to add variety to your talk. Be creative.

Quick Tips

Three S's of Spectacular Speakers

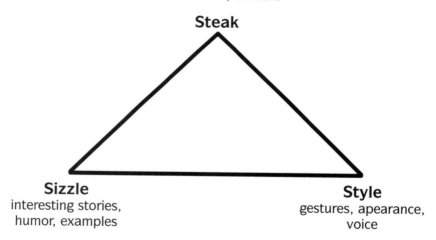

Three S's of Spectacular Speakers

information, content

Steak

Sizzle
interesting stories,
humor, examples

Style
gestures, apearance,
voice

Audience Research Summary

Top three audience requests:

1. Be enthusiastic.
2. Be interesting—use humor and stories.
3. Be knowledgeable—know your stuff.

Steak (the top seven)

Audiences like speakers who:

1. Are knowledgeable—know the topic thoroughly.
2. Are organized. They use a logical and simple format; ideas flow easily.
3. Have a clear message.
4. Focus on the main issues. Get to the point.
5. Present points that are clear and memorable.
6. Are prepared.
7. Give the audience some how-to ideas.

Sizzle (the top eight)

Audiences say:

1. Use humor. Have fun.
2. Be interesting. Do something creative.
3. Tell stories.
4. Relate your message to the audience.
5. Use audience participation.
6. Relay personal anecdotes.
7. Give real-life examples.
8. Be entertaining.

Style (the top eight)

Audiences want:

1. Enthusiasm
2. Confidence
3. A dynamic personality
4. Sincerity
5. A strong and commanding voice
6. Passion
7. Voice fluctuations
8. An articulate presenter

Ten Terrible Turn-offs (in order)

1. Having a monotone voice
2. Reading

3. Boring, uninteresting
4. The "and-uh" syndrome (uh, um, you know . . .)
5. Lack of preparation: being unorganized, rambling, becoming sidetracked
6. Nervous habits: fidgeting, swaying, annoying body language
7. Speaking too long, going overtime
8. Repeating, repeating, repeating
9. Not making eye contact
10. Not relating to the audience: no audience involvement, not tuned in to the audience's needs

Know Your Audience: Information Guide

✓ How many people are there?
✓ What is the age range?
✓ Male or female?
✓ What are their responsibilities and job titles?
✓ Have they heard presenters on this topic before?
✓ What is their interest in your topic?
✓ How much do they know about the subject?
✓ What is their experience in this area?
✓ What do they need to know about it?
✓ What are their top three concerns/needs regarding this topic?
✓ How much do you know about their probable questions and concerns?
✓ Are they in agreement with you?
✓ Who are the decision makers?
✓ What are their expectations?
✓ What are their hobbies and interests?
✓ Are there any current "hot buttons" at work?
✓ Are there any sensitive issues?
✓ If you are speaking in another part of the country or another country, what special factors do you need to consider?
✓ Are there any community issues you should be aware of?
✓ What do they expect you to wear?
✓ What types of stories and examples would work best with this audience?

Style Checklist

- ✓ Gestures: Lively and comfortable, avoided getting stuck in one position
- ✓ Smile (lots of it)
- ✓ Eye contact: Three- to five-second mini-conversations
- ✓ Voice: Lively and energetic
- ✓ Pause: Used lots of pauses effectively
- ✓ Volume: Appropriate for the size of the group
- ✓ Volume: Varied loud and soft
- ✓ Appeared confident
- ✓ Avoided distracting mannerisms
- ✓ Whole body movement: Used the space well; did not pace
- ✓ Facial expression: The face was a messenger for the message, not stone-faced
- ✓ Appearance: Stood out among the crowd; appropriately dressed, used good color, quality; accessory drew attention to the face (tie, bold jewelry)

Summarize:
Two greatest strengths?

1. _____

2. _____

Two greatest weaknesses?

1. _____

2. _____

Presentation Planner: A Steak and Sizzle Approach

Audience Focus

Objective: I want the audience to . . . (to learn? to buy? to laugh? to act?)

Message: (In one sentence, what do I want the audience to remember?)

Audience Considerations: (How can I relate this message to this audience?)

The Presentation

Introduction

GRABM (Grab the audience's attention)
WIFM (Connect with the audience—explain what's in it for them?)
PREVIEW ("Today I'm going to talk about . . .")

Body Alternate steak and sizzle at least every six minutes. Steak is the information, content. Sizzle is the creative part: stories, humor, audience involvement, examples, props.

1. Point 1 and subpoints: steak, sizzle, steak, sizzle . . .
2. Point 2 and subpoints: steak, sizzle, steak, sizzle . . .
3. Point 3 and subpoints: steak, sizzle, steak, sizzle . . .

Conclusion

SUMMARIZE ("To summarize, . . ." "To wrap it up, . . ." "Before I go . . .")
WIFM again!
GRABM again!

Persuasive Presentation Outline (selling products, services, or ideas)

The secret to persuasion is to answer these three questions:

1. What is the buying trigger?
2. What is the buyer looking for?
3. How can I fill that need?

The Presentation

GRABM
WIFM
PREVIEW
IDENTIFY AND ACKNOWLEDGE THE BUYING TRIGGERS/NEEDS

KEY ISSUES: Discuss each need and how you can fulfill the need.

EXAMPLES/SIZZLE: Give examples for each issue.

OTHER DETAILS: Add any other pertinent information.

ANSWER QUESTIONS

SUMMARY: List each need and how you will fulfill it.

WIFM

GRABM

REQUEST FOR ACTION

Ten Ways to Handle Nervousness

1. Never say "nervous." Call it "the Force." Think of an athlete's adrenaline, of being "pumped up" to do a great job.
2. Think positive thoughts.
3. Learn how to look calm. Smile, be yourself, act like you know what you're doing, take your time.
4. Soothe your symptoms. Know how you react during moments of stress, and then see if you can do something about it. Drink water for a dry throat, practice relaxation techniques for a pounding heart, breathe deeply when you are out of breath.
5. Relax. Use deep breathing, practice positive visualization, listen to relaxing music, fill your head with a feeling of "can do."
6. Prepare. Rehearse, practice, anticipate questions, have simplified notes, test the audiovisual equipment, make a checklist of materials and supplies, arrive early.
7. Focus on the audience, not on yourself.
8. Know that you are human. You will make mistakes. The audience will forgive you as long as you apologize once, and then get on with the show.
9. Carefully choose what you eat and drink before a presentation.
10. Exercise.

Master Checklist

- ✓ I know a lot about this audience and their needs.
- ✓ I have tailord my presentation to those needs.
- ✓ The material is organized into three to five main points—clear and simple.
- ✓ I will start and end my talk with a GRABM.
- ✓ I'm using a variety of sizzle every six minutes.
- ✓ I have a simple, one-sentence message that I'll repeat six times.
- ✓ My message has a tie-in to the job/real world/this particular audience.
- ✓ My summary starts with a cue such as "to wrap it up," and it contains my one-sentence message.
- ✓ My audiovisuals are large and can be seen throughout the room.
- ✓ I will test the audiovisual equipment.
- ✓ I have a plan in case the A-V equipment fails.
- ✓ My notes are large and simple.
- ✓ I feel enthusiastic about the topic.
- ✓ I will convey enthusiasm through voice energy, lively gestures, and facial expression.
- ✓ I will use great eye contact: three- to five-second mini-conversations.
- ✓ I plan to arrive early so that I can make any necessary changes in the room.
- ✓ I know how to shrink my presentation if needed.
- ✓ I know how to expand my presentation if needed.
- ✓ I am filling my head with positive thoughts.
- ✓ I am practicing deep breathing regularly.
- ✓ I've rehearsed my presentation several times, using my actual notes and audiovisuals.
- ✓ I am thinking about the audience more than about myself. I know the presentation will benefit them.
- ✓ I've thought about the twenty questions I'm most likely to be asked, and I know how to answer them.
- ✓ I'm looking forward to this presentation, and I plan to make it enjoyable for the audience.

Recommended Resources

Creative Training Techniques Newsletter, Lakewood Publications, 50 S. Ninth St., Minneapolis, MN 55402; (800) 707-7749.

The Executive Speechwriter Newsletter, Words, Ink, Emerson Falls Business Park, St. Johnsbury, VT 05819; (802) 748-4472.

Inspiration Software, 7412 SW Beaverton Hillsdale Highway, Suite 102, Portland, OR 97225; (800) 877-4292.

National Speakers Association, 1500 South Priest Drive, Tempe, AZ 85281; (602) 968-2552.

Glass, Lillian, Ph.D. *Talk to Win: Six Steps to a Successful Vocal Image.* New York: Perigee Books, 1987.

Hoff, Ron. *I Can See You Naked.* Kansas City: Andrews and McMeel, 1988.

Mandel, Steve. *Technical Presentation Skills.* Los Altos, Calif.: Crisp Pub., 1988.

Nelson, Robert B. *Louder and Funnier.* Berkeley, Calif.: Ten Speed Press, 1985.

Peoples, David A. *Presentations Plus.* New York: John Wiley & Sons, 1988.

Van Ekeren, Glenn. *The Speaker's Sourcebook: Quotes, Stories, and Anecdotes for Every Occasion.* Englewood Cliffs, N.J.: Prentice-Hall, 1988.

Walters, Dottie, and Lilly Walters. *Speak and Grow Rich.* Englewood Cliffs, N.J.: Prentice-Hall, 1989.

Wilder, Claudyne. *The Presentations Kit: 10 Steps for Selling Your Ideas.* New York: John Wiley & Sons, 1990.

Index

activity
  change in, 107–108
  ideas for, 49
adaptability, 15–17
aerobics, face, 71
anchoring message, 36–37
appearance, 6, 136–137
  evaluation of, 73
  for men, 63–65
  for women, 65–67
athlete, eating like, 60
attention grabber, 28, 31–32
attire, 136–137
  for men, 64–65
  for women, 65–67
audience
  activation of, 49–50
  captivating with steak, sizzle,
    and style, 6
  checking pulse of, 100–101
  connecting with, 13–24
  conversation with, 105–106
  desire of, for "sizzle," 10–11
  desire of, for "steak," 10
  desire of, for "style," 11
  with different knowledge lev-
    els, 140
  falling asleep, 59
  finding common ground with,
    44–45
  focus on, 28–29, 58–59, 145–146
  getting in synch with, 17–18
  holding attention of, 133
  ignoring speaker, 3
  informant on, 14–15
  interest of, in speaker, 62
  involving, 107
  knowledge of, 14, 144
  large, 139
  listening to, 5–6
  not relating to, 8
  observation of, 138
  participation of, 6, 10, 107
  politeness of, 3
  rapport with, 138
  reenergizing of, 105–106
  regaining interest of, 132–133
  relating to, 10–11, 125–126
  research results on, 142–144
  stepping into shoes of, 15–17
  survey questionnaire of, 4–5
  technical and nontechnical, 9
  ten turn-offs of, 7–9, 143–144
  top three requests of, 142
  understanding of, 133–134
audiovisual aids, 72
  see also visual aids
audiovisual equipment failure,
    59–60
authority, interesting or unusual,
    43

Blanchard, Ken
    self-disclosure of, 47
    theme of, 21
"Boring Person's Guidelines to
    Humor," 50
Bradshaw, John, vocal variety of,
    82
break(s)
    snack, 108
    taking, 102–103
breathing, in voice control, 75–76
Brooks, Garth, on preparing for
    audience, 16
business attire
    for men, 64
    for women, 65
buying trigger, 37
buzz groups, 107

Carson, Johnny, style of, 21
charisma factor, enhancement of,
    19–20
child, thinking like, 25
clarity, 10, 29–30
colors
    for men, 64
    for women, 65–66
common ground, 20
    finding, 44–45
computer graphics, testing of, 96
computer-generated shows,
    92–94
confidence, 11, 55–56
convincing speech, 82
C.P.R., presentation, 99–109
creative ideas, 25–26
creativity, 9
cue words, 72

dazzle, 46
demonstrations, 44
diet, healthy, 60

distracters, 70–71
duck, behaving like, 55–56

Eber, José, OOMPH of, 21
end early, 103–104
energy, 68–69
    breathing and, 75
    physical, 105
    recovering, 102–104
energy boosters, 105
enthusiasm, 5, 11
    vocal expression of, 81–82
evaluation, style, 73
everyday lives, presentation ef-
    fects on, 18–19
exercise, physical, 60–61
eye contact, 67–68
    evaluation of, 73
    lack of, 8
    pitfalls of, 68
eye-surfing, 68

facial expression
    animated, 71–72
    evaluation of, 73
facilitator, meeting, 118–119
fear, overcoming, 132
fiddling and fidgeting, 70–71
flip charts, 88–90
    in meetings, 118
    testing of, 96
focus, 10
    of audience, 28–29
    on audience, 58–59, 145–146
    creation of, 29–30
    on self, 58

gesture paralysis, 69
gestures, 6
    evaluation of, 73
    importance of, 70

overcoming awkwardness with, 131–132
taking up space with, 69
getting up, 105–106
GRABM, 28, 29, 32–33
group
  activities of, 109
  involvement of, 119
  presentations, 107
  see also audience
gusto, gauging, 79–80

hair
  for men, 65
  for women, 67
handouts, 95
hobby, showcasing of, 48–49
homework, on audience, 17
how-to ideas, 10
how-to tools, 21
humor, 6, 10–11, 22, 50

idea web, 25–26, 27
ideas
  demonstrations of, 44
  to perk up presentation, 108–109
  storyboard for, 35
  that stick, 46, 137
informant, finding, 14–15
information
  questions to help discover, 15
  sources of, 14–15
  as steak, 6
  in visual aids, 85
insider, 17–18
Inspiration Software, 26

jump-starting, 24–25

Kennedy, J. F., as good speaker, 11
knowledge, of audience, 14

knowledgeable speaker, 5, 10

Lansbury, Angela, vocal uniqueness of, 83
laughing together with audience, 22
laughter, 50
lectern, use of, 70
lighting, testing of, 97
likability, 20
listening
  to audience, 5–6
  in meetings, 118

makeup, 67
mannerisms, evaluation of, 73
McKay, Harvey, theme of, 21
meeting leader's pledge, 112
meetings
  alternatives to, 111
  creative and productive, 110–111
  evaluation of, 113, 114–116
  facilitating, 118–119
  fifty-nine-minute, 114, 115
  planning for, 112–113
  quick and snappy, 112–114
  rating style of, 121–122
  reason for, 111
  responsibilities in, 117
  sizzle in, 116–117
  steak for, 112
  sticky situations in, 119–121
Memorable Speaker Survey, 41
message, 6, 29
  anchoring of, 36–37
  checking audience's understanding of, 133–134
  connecting, to audience, 15–16
microphone, testing of, 96
monotone voice, 7–8
mood, audience, 16–17

motivating speech, 82
motivational speaker, for high
    school audience, 123–126
motor-mouths, 22
movement, 6, 68–69
    distracting, 70–71
    variety of, 72
    see also gestures

name dropping, 46–47
nervous habits, 7, 8
nervousness
    control of, 53–61
    diet and, 60
    exercise to calm, 60–61
    soothing, 56
    as "the force," 54
    ways to handle, 147
Nike sales managers workshop,
    18
notes
    directing eyes to, 68
    easy-to-follow, 59
    keeping simple, 35–36
    throwing out, 106
    use of, 135–136

"on" buttons, activation of, 18–19
The One-Minute Manager (Blanch-
    ard), 47
OOMPH, development of, 20–21
Oregon State Bar Continuing
    Legal Education, 3
outgoing personality, 11
overhead projector, testing of, 96
overhead transparencies
    cluttered *vs.* uncluttered, 88
    control of, 91–92
    supercharged, 90–91
    three-point arrangement for, 94

pacing, 139
    change in, 107–108

Palmer, Arnold, vocal uniqueness
    of, 83
panic, avoiding of, 59–60
passion, 11
    vocal expression of, 81–82
pauses
    in meetings, 118
    to punctuate point, 80–81
    silent, 78
Peoples, David, on visual aids, 85
Perot, Ross, vocal impression of,
    76
personalization, 63
persuasion, planning for, 37–38
persuasive presentation outline,
    146–147
Peters, Tom
    speaking from heart, 81
    style of, 21
Pickering, Wayne, theme of, 21
pitch, of voice, 78–79
planning, 27–29
    for persuasion, 37–38
    pre-meeting, 112–113
podium, use of, 70
points
    jazzing up, 31–32
    punctuating with pause, 80–81
    selection of, 30–31
    sticking to, 138
posture, 69–70
positive thoughts, 54–55
power colors
    for men, 64
    for women, 65–66
practice methods, 134–135
preparation, 10, 134
    checklist for, 57–58
    lack of, 8
presentation
    C.P.R. for, 99–109
    enjoyment in, 138–139

master checklist for, 148
organization of, 24–38
panic over, 53–61
planning for, 146
reading, 7, 8
presentation planner, 28, 145–146
presentation skills
  defining strategy for developing, 4–5
  reminder to work on, 136
Presentations Plus (Peoples), 85
preview, 32–33
problem, pinpointing of, 101–102
problem solving
  activity for, 107
  facilitator's guide to, 119
products, demonstration of, 44
projector
  failure of, 97
  setup of, 93
  testing of, 96
props, 46

qualities
  categories of, 6
  of good speaker, 5
  quality circles, 119
  questionnaire, audience survey, 4–5
  questions, answering with confidence, 135
  quick tips, 142–148
  quotations, 43

Raphael, Sally Jesse, OOMPH of, 21
rapport, developing, 138
real-life examples, 10–11, 42–43
relaxation, 57
relevance, to audience, 10–11, 18
responsibilities, meeting, 117
rhythm, speech, 82

Robbins, Anthony, reenergizing techniques of, 105
Robertson, Jeannie, OOMPH of, 21
role model
  for men, 65
  for women, 67
room setup, testing of, 96

scene-stealers, 23
Scharenbroich, Mark, motivational style, 123–126
self-disclosure, 47–48
selling, *vs.* telling, 37–38
show-and-tell, 44
silent pause, 78
sizzle, 6, 142
  audience requests for, 143
  checking supply of, 33
  every six minutes, 41–50
  importance of, 10–11
  for meetings, 116–117
  in motivational speech to high school kids, 124–125
  planning for, 27–29
  working on, 7
slides, 92–94
  testing of, 96
slip charts, 69
smiling, 71–72
smoking, voice and, 84
snack break, 108
snipes, 23
soothing symptoms, 56
souls, reaching into, 21–22
space, taking up, 68–69
speaker qualities
  categories of, 11–12
  good, 5
Speakers Training Camp
  categories of speaker qualities in, 11–12

Speakers Training Camp
(*continued*)
cornerstone of, 5
typical questions from, 131–141
speaking
from heart, 81–82
rate of, 76–77
Spectacular Speakers, Three S's
of, 142
spectacular speaker's triangle, 6
speech
changing speed of, 76–77, 107
expanding, 137
long, 7, 8
pauses in, 80–81
rhythm of, 82
Spence, Jerry, OOMPH of, 21
spotlight, stepping out of, 107
steak, 6, 142
audience requests for, 143
importance of, 10
for meetings, 112
in motivational speech to high
school kids, 124
organization in, 24–38
planning for, 27–29
stories, 6, 10–11, 42–43
overused, 43
related to audience, 19
storyboarding, 34–35
strategy, for developing presentation skills, 4–5
style, 6, 21, 62–67, 137–138, 142
audience requests for, 143
changing, 104
checklist for, 145
evaluation of, 73
importance of, 11
in meetings, 121–122
in motivational speech to high
school kids, 125
stretching, 72–73
working on, 7

summary, memorable, 33
surprises, 133

team spirit, 111
technical audience, speaker qualities desired by, 9
themes, 21
thoughts
positive, 54–55
provoking new, 21
timing, 139
topic ruts, 19
troublemakers, taming of, 22–23
turn-offs
avoidance of, 7–9
ten terrible, 143–144

"uh" syndrome, 7, 8
getting rid of, 77–78
uniqueness, development of, 137

VCR, testing of, 96
video presentation, 92–94
visual aids
benefits of, to audience, 85
benefits of, to presenter, 85–86
cluttered, 86–87, 88
computer/video, 92–94
control of, 91–92
failure of, 97–98
reasons, can't be seen, 89
reinforcing, 95
simple, 86
spontaneous, 88–90
supercharged, 90–91
tailored to audience, 140–141
testing of, 96–97
variety of, 72
visible, 87
visualization
of favorite place, 57
of positive situation, 55

vocal garbage, 77–78
voice
    assessing strengths and weak-
      nesses of, 83–84
    boring, 140
    breathing and, 75–76
    commanding, 11
    controls of, 74–75
    evaluation of, 73
    female, 78
    fluctuations of, 11
    gusto of, 79–80
    impressions from, 74

    monotone, 7–8
    pitch of, 78–79
    speed of, 76–77
    taking care of, 84
    uniqueness of, 83–84
    volume of, 79–80

whoops factor, 47–48
WIFMs (What's in it for me?), 32
    in summary, 33
writing devices, testing of, 96–97

Zigler, Zig, speaking rate of, 77